//
Growing Food in the Super Grand Solar Minimum

It's Not You – It's not CO2 – It's the Sun

Author – Dennis DeLaurier

Growing Food in the Super Grand Solar Minimum is Copyright © 2019 by Dennis DeLaurier All Rights Reserved.

All rights reserved. No part of this book may be reproduced in any form or by any electronic or mechanical means including information storage and retrieval systems, without permission in writing from the author. The only exception is by a reviewer, who may quote short excerpts in a review.

Cover designed by Dennis DeLaurier

Graphics:

It's is almost impossible to write a book on many diverse growing systems and types without pictures and graphics.

All graphics used in this book have been purchased or actually created by the author. Other graphics are public domain or are part of the collaborative global commons. CC 2.0 or greater. Additional graphics are used with the permission of commercial agriculture equipment companies which have granted permission for use in this book. All such graphics will have a link back to the company's source or website.

Dedication

This book is dedicated to my family who I hope with some planning and preparation will survive the coming Super Grand Solar Minimum and global cooling on the horizon.

You may visit My Blog on the here and now Super Grand Solar Minimum by clicking here at this URL which will take you to my Surviving The Super Grand Solar Minimum Blog

Table of CONTENTS

Welcome 4
Systems that use electrical power 5
Electrical Power and water is a safety hazard 6
pH and EC 14
Hydroponic NFT 16
    Home Made Systems 17
    Small Commercial Systems 18
    How to grow in an NFT Tray 19
Hydroponic Ebb and Flow 24
    Culture Tank System 24
    Two Container System 25
Aeriation system 29
    The Bubble Machine 30
    The 1 Gallon Bubbler System 32
Aeroponic Systems 34
    Mister Cloner 36
    Commercial Systems 41
Drip systems 43
    2 Box Dripper 44
    Dip Stick Special 50
Aquaponics System 56
Float and Raft Systems 59
    Soda-Pop Special 60
    Commercial Float Systems 64
Non Electrical Systems 65
    Grow Bags 66
    Tips Using Grow Bags 74
Kratky method 76
Gardens and Gardening 87
    Raised Beds 88
    Straw Bed Gardening – Hay Bed Gardening 91
    Ruth Stout Garden 93
    Homework 96
    Square Foot Gardening 98
    Hugelkultur raised bed 101
Microgreen Growing 103
Vertical Gardening Ideas 112
Growing Potatoes 113
Growing Carrots 116
Growing Jerusalem Artichokes 118
Greenhouses 120

    Greenhouses – Build your own..121
Hydroponic Nutrients 123
Information on the Author – Dennis DeLaurier..124

Welcome

If you have never grown your own food, I hope this book will help you get started. The Super Grand Solar Minimum will make growing and purchasing food problematic at best. As our global food growing systems fail and the planet cools, it will at some point become difficult to purchase food grown by others. That is the reason for this book. When it comes to food security, the best security is to grow food in multiple ways. If one fails, then the other will possibly still provide you with food. Because of the many elements that make up the SGSM, there are all types of social and environmental problems that put your food growing at peril. It is with these ideas in mind that I offer you this book. Hopefully you will find something useful.

Approach:

My approach to growing my own food is to operate in the following environments and conditions.

- System that use electrical power
- Small Commercial systems
- Systems that do not use electrical power
- System that are inside
- Systems that are outside
- Systems that are protected and unprotected
- Systems that are stealth grown
- Cold weather systems
- Hot weather systems
- Soil Based growing
- Extreme cold weather growing
- Grow Bags
- Vertical Towers
- Kratky Method and no or low energy growing.

The above could almost be endless, and there is just so much I can put in this book, I will try to put the best of what is out there and hopefully you can find something useful.

In this book you will find many diverse types of growing systems of which many of have been used successfully by the author on a 5 ½ acre farm in Central Texas.

Systems that use electrical power

There are a huge numbers of food growing systems that use electrical power. Usually the electricity is used to operate some sort of a pump that delivers nutrients to the plants or air to the plant roots. These systems can be the following:

- Hydroponic NFT
- Hydroponic Ebb and Flow
- Aeriation system
- Drip system
- Aeroponics systems
- Aquaponics Systems
- Float and Raft Systems

You will find all this below, but before you jump in and get your hands wet, you need to think pH and EC. Also because you will be using electricity, you need to think about safety and especially electrical safety.

You are in luck because such a chapter is provided below.

Electrical Power and water is a safety hazard

Don't ignore this Chapter. Working with water and submerge pumps and electrical timers and other electrical devices can cause injury or even death if ignored. We don't want you pushing up daisies before the SGSM even gets here.

Below is my often used section on electrical safety.

Note: This is NOT an Electrical Safety Course

DO NOT USE ANY OF THE INFORMATION IN THIS SECTION AS SAFETY TRAINING, AS THEY ARE ONLY SUGGESTIONS. TAKE A COURSE IN CPR AND ELECTRICAL SAFETY. YOUR LOCAL POWER COMPANY MAY ASSIST YOU. SEEK PROFESSIONAL TRAINING.

- Concepts Covered in this Chapter
- Causes of electrical shock
- Current paths through the body
- Effects of electrical current on the body
- Safety precautions when working with electricity
- Fuses circuit breakers and other safety equipment

Working with electricity and liquids can be dangerous if you do not understand the risks. Because hydroponics is so much fun, we seldom think about any of the hazards associated with our equipment. It is the intent of this module to get you thinking about these risks and suggest that you become aware of electrical hazards by educating yourself, and making sure that all your equipment and power sources meet all the electrical codes that the state, county and city will require. Even meeting the standards is no guarantee of safety, if you do not take electrical safety seriously. This module is not a course on electrical safety. That sort of training is your responsibility and we strongly suggest that you seek out professional training in this area if you think you need it.

The following is a list of important suggestions and information that should be taken seriously:

- Electricity can cause serious harm or death, always take it seriously.
- If you are unsure, ask an expert.
- Know where the fire extinguisher is located.
- Never work on wet floors
- Always turn off power before making repairs or disassembling equipment.
- If your equipment is defective, cease operation and repair it or discard it.
- Never work alone when working around hazardous voltages.

- Before starting work, familiarize yourself with the location of circuit breakers, and power receptacles for all equipment.

More good suggestions

- Be sure that all equipment which has a metal case or metal knobs is grounded by way of a 3-wire cable.
- Do not work with damaged equipment! Never remove plugs by pulling on the cords.
- Before touching any wiring or high voltage points be sure that the power is turned off!
- Always wear shoes and never work when wet.
- If you are not sure a circuit is energized, assume that it is and check with a meter. Never take anyone's word that the power has been turned off.
- Never touch or work with equipment that is immersed in liquids: Example, turn off power if you must work with your nutrient pump.

Electrical shock occurs when we become a path between an electrical source.

You can suffer an electric shock indoors or out, whether it's from accidentally touching a frayed electric cord, working on electrical or electronic equipment or being struck by lightning. Even a mild shock can cause burns and a major shock can be fatal.

Fatal Current

Electrocution can occur when a very small electrical current flows through the heart for 1 to 3 seconds. It only takes between 6-200 mA (milliamperes) of current flowing through the heart to disrupt the normal coordination of heart muscles. These muscles lose their vital rhythm and begin to fibrillate. Death can soon follow if something is not done.

"Death can soon follow if something is not done."

As an informed person, there is a lot that can be done. Here is what you can do.

Go and take a CPR lesson, and keep your certification up to date.

Before working with a shock victim, you must remove the source from the victim's body if necessary. This could be as easy as turning off the power. Never touch another shock victim unless there is no longer a shock danger to your person. If there are others present, have them call 911 (in Australia it is 000) while you apply CPR. Check for breathing and signs of a good heart rhythm. No matter what your location, It is a good idea to have emergency numbers posted or in your wallet or purse.

DO NOT USE ANY OF THE INFORMATION IN THIS MODULE AS SAFETY TRAINING, AS THEY ARE ONLY SUGGESTIONS. TAKE A COURSE IN CPR AND ELECTRICAL SAFETY. YOUR LOCAL POWER COMPANY MAY ASSIST YOU. SEEK PROFESSIONAL TRAINING.

Now that we have discussed shock, there may be those who will say "I have been shocked, and I am still alive". The answer to that may be that you are just lucky! It is possible to receive a very nasty shock and escape injury or death. Here is what happens when the body comes in contact with a live circuit.

First, the live circuit may not have the capacity to push 6 to 200 mA through your body and heart. You probably have been shocked by static electricity when walking across carpets or removed clothing from your clothes dryer. These voltages could be as high as 20 to 30 THOUSAND volts. The reason you are still here is there is little current involved, and it is current that stops the heart. You probably know that a good conductor can support high current. Under normal conditions, your body is a fair conductor, but if you have touched a live (powerful) circuit, it can actually burn your skin and then you will conduct current even better. Once the normal resistance of your body is removed, current can increase.

Shock Review

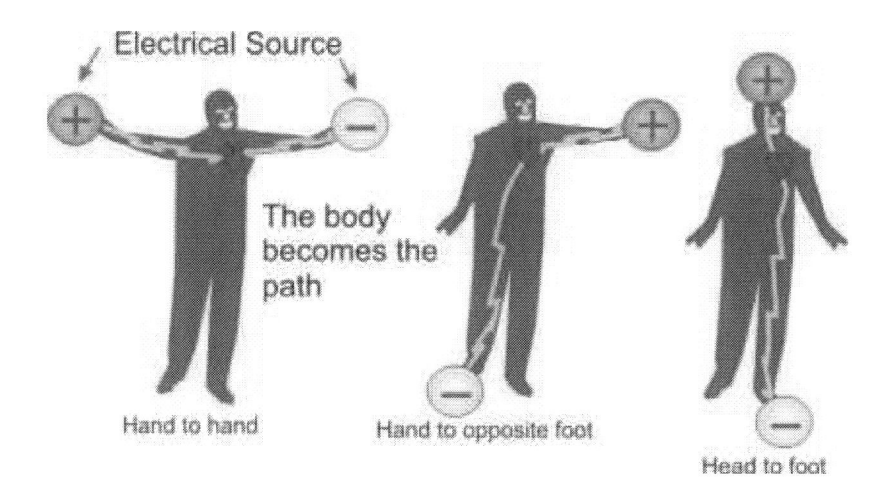

Electrical Source
The body becomes the path
Hand to hand
Hand to opposite foot
Head to foot

Currents as little as 6 to 200 mA can cause the heart to cease its normal rhythm.

When the body comes in contact with a voltage that source must have enough potential to cause current flow through the body and heart.

The body at first has some resistance to current flow, but an electrical burn can cause this resistance to be lowered and the body then becomes a better conductor.

Electrical shock can also cause burns and muscle damage. For an electrical shock to be fatal requires that the current goes through the heart and affects the heart muscle which controls the heart rhythm. When this happens, the heart goes into fibrillation.

Fatal Current Paths (see pic above)

There are three major pathways through the heart that can be fatal. These are from hand to hand, hand to opposite foot and head to foot. Note that all three of these paths are through the heart. If the path is not through the heart it could cause severe shock, burns to the body and muscle damage

Now that you understand what electrical shock does to the body and the paths that an electrical shock may be fatal, it will become much easier when working with dangerous voltages. You do not have to go to work to find dangerous voltages, as your house has them in every room. The 120 volt wall plug has a current capacity of perhaps 15 amps! Many people are electrocuted each year from house hold voltages. The main thing that you must never do is to come in contact with these sources when you are working with and around them.

That is why equipment must always be grounded. If a high voltage was shorted to a metal equipment chassis or case and there were no ground, then the case would become hot! Obviously some circuits and voltage are more dangerous than others. Your 1 ½ volt battery or 9 volt radio battery are not very dangerous as they have little potential to move enough current through your body. BUT, even a very low voltage like your 12 volt car battery when shorted can cause heat and cause burns.

Conclusion

- Work smart and know and understand the dangers.
- Never work with ungrounded equipment
- Never modify or remove a ground from a cord or piece of equipment.
- Never work alone when working with dangerous voltages.
- When making a repair always turn off the power.
- Always ASSUME the circuit is energized until you know differently.
- Always check a circuit with a volt meter to see if the circuit is hot.
- ALWAYS remove rings, watches and other metal jewelry when working on any type of equipment or electrical circuit.
- Use common sense and be concerned not just about yourself, but others around you. Work as a team if possible.

Three-to-two prong adaptor plugs are not recommended

Power cord with ground prong cut off.

Most homes will have three-conductor receptacles that accommodate electrical cords with three-prong plugs. The third (round) prong provides a path to ground. Most modern electronic equipment have three-prong plugs.

Also, never use a power cord which has the third prong (ground) cut (see graphic above.

Another device called a GFCI is a device that can prevent electrical shock. The Ground Fault Circuit Interrupter or GFCI. provides power much like the standard three connection wall socket, but are normally installed in areas where electricity and water could mix. You will probably find these devices at home in your bathroom, laundry room, kitchen, and outdoors. It is also a good idea to have these devices available when powering your electrical hydroponics equipment. In fact, many of the pumps used in hydroponics call for using these devices.

These devices sense any (very small) current to ground, and open up the circuit very quickly before any damage or injury can occur. As shown above the GFCI has buttons that are marked Test and Reset.

It is a good idea to test the GFCI at least monthly. If the GFCI is triggered, remove the load, and press the reset button. You might want to look at the equipment that caused the GFCI to trip.

In Australia, GFCIs are called RCDs (Residual Current Devices) and all homes must come equipped with one at the service box.

Ceramic Fuse   Circuit Breaker

Most electrical and electronic devices when operating properly do not use excessive current and will operate normally with standard AC circuits in our homes or at work. If the equipment becomes shorted or defective, it could start using excessive current and lf there were no overload protection on the line or in the equipment, this overload could cause a fire or injury. To stop excessive current flow, the equipment might have a fuse. If your electrical power distribution is up to code, it will be distributed through a circuit breaker.

Fuses have a voltage and current rating. A fuse has a small wire or conductor that melt if excessive current flows through the fuse. This "opens" the circuit and removes the voltage from the load.

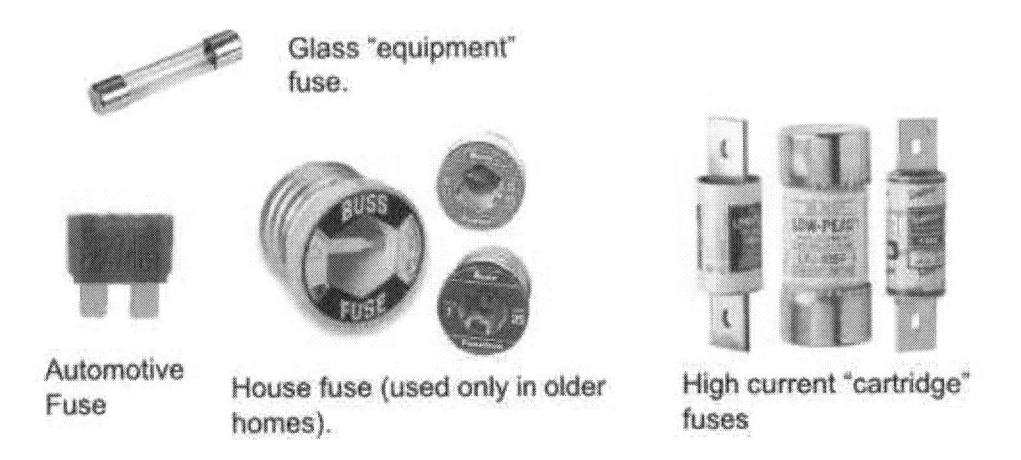

Glass "equipment" fuse.

Automotive Fuse   House fuse (used only in older homes).   High current "cartridge" fuses

When a fuse blows, the process destroys the fuse, and it must be replaced. A solution to this problem is a resettable device called a Circuit Breaker. A circuit breaker passes current through a special bimetallic strip that coils or bends when excessive current heats up the strip. The strip then breaks the circuit. Most modern homes and businesses use this type of breaker and are installed in a circuit breaker panel as shown above. The panel supplies power for different parts of the home or business. If the breaker is tripped, it must manually be reset. If the circuit still has excessive current being drawn, it will trip again.

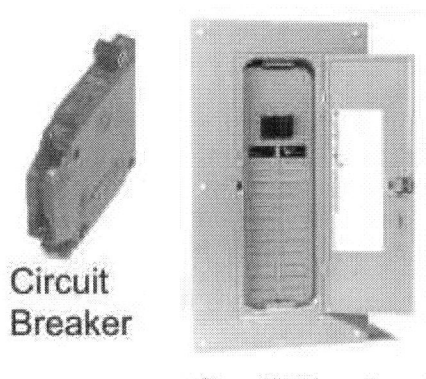

Circuit Breaker

Circuit Breaker Panel

Breaker like fuses are voltage and current rated.

Be safe; get safety and especially electrical training

Information contained in this book is offered as is and has been obtained from sources believed to be reliable by the author. However, the author does not guarantee the accuracy or completeness of any information offered and published herein. The author shall not be responsible for any errors, omissions or damages arising out of use of this information. This book is released with the understanding that the author is not attempting to render engineering or other professional services. If such services are required, the assistance of the appropriate professional should be sought.

Note: in some areas and countries it is illegal to do your own electrical work and for good reason. Make sure you follow all local, state and other laws and codes when it comes to installing or repairing your electrical service.

Finally if you are using direct power connections order and use one of these if there is no GFCI protector. This is an inline one.

SAFETY FIRST

Safety Starts Here

Think Safe...
Work Safe...
Be Safe

pH and EC

pH and EC are two important factors that can cause plant growth problems. Let's look at pH first.

When working with plants, pH is a scale used to specify how acidic or basic a water-based solution is. Acidic solutions have a lower pH, while basic solutions have a higher ph. At room temperature pure water is neither acidic nor basic and has a pH of 7. While you can go crazy with pH, just make sure that your *nutrient and water is around 6.5, and quit worrying!* While you can spend a bunch of money measuring pH using a fancy meter with a digital readout but the best and less expensive way is to use test strips as shown below. Note the list of recommended pH and EC (Electrical Conductivity) values.

Just dip the strip in your water or nutrient and then match up the color on the strip container. Really simple.

Crops	EC (mS)	pH
Asparagus	1.9 - 2.5	6.0 - 6.8
Basil	1.4 - 2.2	5.5 - 6.5
Broccoli	3.8 - 4.8	6.0 - 6.8
Cabbage	3.4 - 4.1	6.5 - 7.0
Carrots	2.2 - 2.8	6.3
Cucumber	2.4 - 3.4	5.5
Eggplant	3.4 - 4.8	6.0
Garlic	2.0 - 2.5	6.0
Lettuce	1.1 - 1.7	6.0 - 7.0
Mint	2.8 - 3.3	6.5 - 7.0
Rosemary	1.4 - 2.2	6.0 - 7.5
Sage	1.4 - 2.2	6.0 - 6.5
Spinach	2.5 - 3.2	6.0 - 7.0
Strawberries	2.5 - 3.1	6.0
Thyme	1.1 - 2.2	6.5 - 7.0
Tomatoes	2.8 - 7.0	6.0 - 6.5

OK, so what do you do if you pH is too high or too low? You can purchase a bottle of **pH UP or pH DOWN** At your hydroponic store as shown below. This is what the author uses.

pH Down – Keep away from children.

OK, What about EC (Electrical Conductivity). Hydroponic fertilizers (nutrients) are made up of various salts (chemicals) that your plants will need. Because you are not growing in the ground, you will need to provide everything the plant will need to grow. When you mix these salts or use premixes, the solution will conduct electricity. That is what an EC meter does. I have grown vegetables not even caring about EC as I was mixing them with pH balanced water and used the amounts recommended with the purchased commercial nutrients. During the SGSM, you probably won't be using battery powered equipment anyway. Just make sure about once a month replace the nutrients with fresh ones. So if you don't have the money to purchase a meter, then the best thing you can do is use the recommended mixture that came with the instructions. Below is the Authors Bluelab EC meter. Expensive but worth it. I have had mine for many years with great results.

Crops	EC (mS)	pH
Asparagus	1.9 - 2.5	6.0 - 6.8
Basil	1.4 - 2.2	5.5 - 6.5
Broccoli	3.8 - 4.8	6.0 - 6.8
Cabbage	3.4 - 4.1	6.5 - 7.0
Carrots	2.2 - 2.8	6.3
Cucumber	2.4 - 3.4	5.5
Eggplant	3.4 - 4.8	6.0
Garlic	2.0 - 2.5	6.0
Lettuce	1.1 - 1.7	6.0 - 7.0
Mint	2.8 - 3.3	6.5 - 7.0
Rosemary	1.4 - 2.2	6.0 - 7.5
Sage	1.4 - 2.2	6.0 - 6.5
Spinach	2.5 - 3.2	6.0 - 7.0
Strawberries	2.5 - 3.1	6.0
Thyme	1.1 - 2.2	6.5 - 7.0
Tomatoes	2.8 - 7.0	6.0 - 6.5

I could spend a huge amount of this book on what goes into a hydroponic nutrient. I suggest that if that is important to you then do some research.

Hydroponic NFT

There are huge amounts of greens grown in NFT systems all over the planet.

Nutrient Film Technique (NFT)
In a NFT system, plant roots are bathed in a continuous flow of nutrients. Nutrients are recycled. The water used to make up the nutrients are usually Ph adjusted.

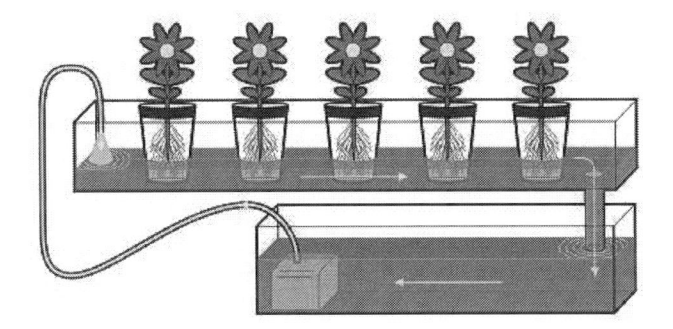

NFT System

The basic principle of a nutrient film technique system is that the roots of plants have access to a constantly running and very shallow stream (film) of nutrient solution flowing down an enclosed gutter.

The flow of nutrient is controlled by a pump that is submerged in a nutrient tank. The pump runs continuously and provides liquids and oxygen to the plants roots. Plants are placed in the gutter trough through holes cut in the top of the gutter. This allows the roots of the plant to sit on the bottom of the gutter and into the nutrient stream. The gutter is set up so the return tube is lower than the rest of the system. Gravity then allows the nutrient to return to the nutrient tank.

Commercial Systems below growing Lettuce.

Home Made Systems

Below on the left is a home brew system NFT system using rain gutter. On the right is a home brew PVC pipe system growing lettuce.

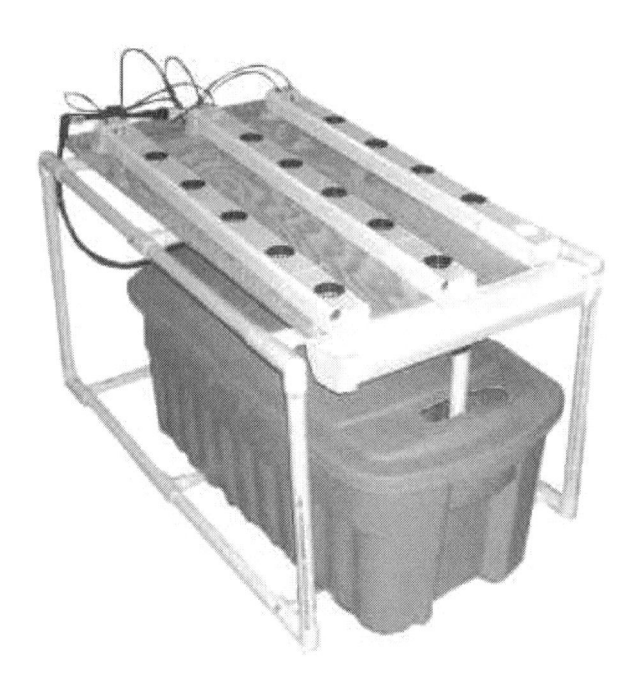

I have grown for many years using NFT systems. While most systems use a continuous feed of nutrients to the plants, this is not a necessity especial for home users of a NFT System. It is quite possible to run the pump for 5 minutes every hour and the plants would be very happy. I agree that a commercial grower would not do that, but I have grown many different types of veggies using this method. The only requirement that you would have is that **you would be growing in cubes that absorb and hold water**.

Small Commercial Systems

There are all types of small commercial NFT systems that could be purchased and would be **ideal** in a home (need grow lights) or in a small greenhouse or outside if the conditions are OK.

If you are not handy at making things, a commercial system is probably ideal. Lettuce, Basil, mustards and other things really grow well in an NFT system. One of the nice things is that many of these vegetables can be picked over time and they will continue to produce. If you are growing greens, **all you will need is a lettuce nutrient.** This will work with most greens like mustards and others. You can purchase these nutrients at your local hydroponic store or online. You can purchase liquid or solid types of nutrients which come as concentrates and are mixed with water. Both work equally well, personally I like the solid types but it's your choice.

Below are two such systems sold by Growers Supply at this URL. The one on the left is a bit smaller than the one on the right. Both would work quite well in the home or in a greenhouse.

Almost any type of plant can be grown in an NFT tray, but some are more practical. Fast growing types are the best as others get too large and take too much time. In the picture below is an example of how large some vegetables can get.

19

How to grow in an NFT Tray

Swiss chard reached for the sky in an NFT Tray

So how do you grow in an NFT tray? The main thing is supporting your starts. They starts can be grown in the Starter Plugs or in soil, cleaned up and transferred into Net Pots. Just make sure the roots are in the stream of nutrients. It's not a good idea to use soil or things like coconut fiber in a NFT system as it will cause a real mess in your nutrient tank.

It pretty easy and here are some of the solutions.

- Net Pots
- Rockwool Starter Plugs
- Clay Pebbles

Net Pots above – fill them with Clay Pebbles alone with starts.

Rockwool Starter Plugs – Grow your starts in these plugs and insert into the NFT trays. (my favorite)

Clay pebbles – place in Net Pot along with start.

Author's basil in a Rockwool Starter Plug in my NFT tray. See below.

Greens grown in an NFT Tray. The nice thing about greens and lettuces is that they may be harvested over time.

Lettuces in a homemade greenhouse growing in NFT Trays.

So what are the advantages of a NFT system? First they can be quite simple. An NFT tray supplies all that is needed for quick growth and can continuously provide you with fresh produce as you can grow your greens at different stages. Harvest when ready, but always have starts ready to grow as you make room for them in the trays. NFT systems do take some attention, but the results are worth it.

Hydroponic Ebb and Flow

(Also known as flood and drain systems)

The Ebb and Flow System, works by temporarily flooding a culture tank containing a growing medium and then draining it. Nutrient is fed to the tank by a pump which is controlled by a timer. The solution is drawn out of the flood tray through the pump, when the pump is turned off. The timer is calibrated to repeat this cycle as many times as necessary. Over watering is prevented by an **overflow tube** that returns excess fluid if the culture tank is over watered. After the pump is turned off, nutrient flows back through the pump. These type of system can be made small (like Mine) or really large. When the system is turned off, oxygen is pulled back into the medium which is usually Clay Pebbles.

Culture Tank System

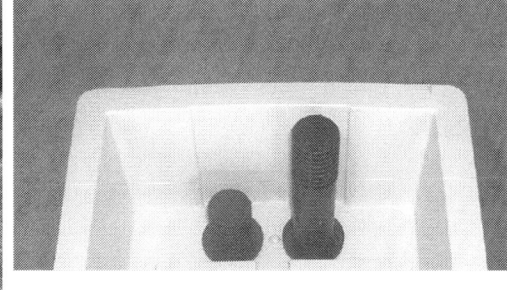

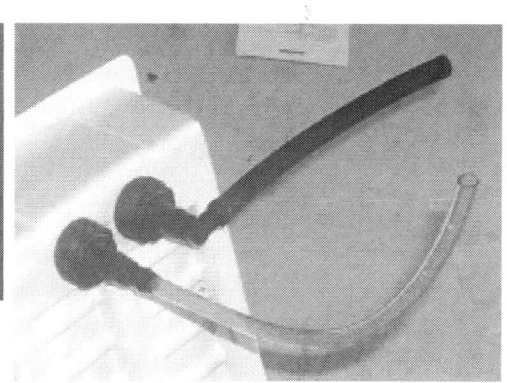

Authors finished system **Nutrient input on left and overflow on right**
Bottom of Culture Tank

Why would the home grower want to use an Ebb and Flow system?

This type of system produces some really good results, and should be considered as a good system to try. Small commercial ebb and flow systems are available for the home and are attractive looking as well. It is possible to order kits and parts to make this system. It is also possible to construct an ebb and flow system using materials at most home centers. A complete system can be built mostly from PVC parts. The ebb and flow system works well because it provides the exact amounts of nutrients to the plants. Large amounts of lettuce, herbs and other vegetables can be grown. Another good point to the ebb and flow system is its low water usage. It is possible to construct very large commercial ebb and flow systems, which confirms how good this type of system works.

Two Container System

Below is a larger system built with two storage containers.

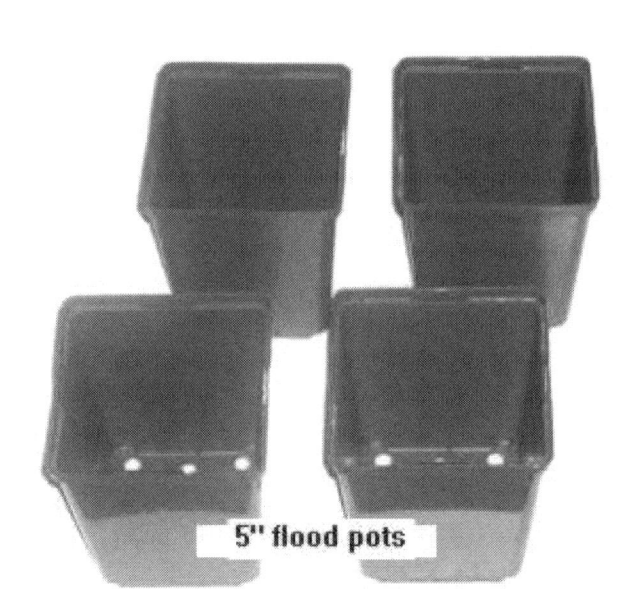

This system is so easy to build and will give wonderful results. It is an ideal system for the beginner. The system is made up of two plastic storage containers the top container is smaller (10 gallon) than the bottom one (14 gallon) that contains the pump and the nutrient. Both of the containers are made by Rubbermaid. As seen from the graphic, the top container holds the four green pots, the flood and drain fixtures and a plastic matrix that keeps the four pots off the bottom of the container and allows for complete draining between flood cycles.

Pieces and Parts

An ebb and flow system is an active system that has a flood tray that is periodically flooded with nutrient. In this design, a small aquarium pump is used. It only pumps 80 GPH, but works very well. I found this pump in a large pet supply shop. Both of the containers were purchased at Target for less than $5.00. The pump was around $12.00

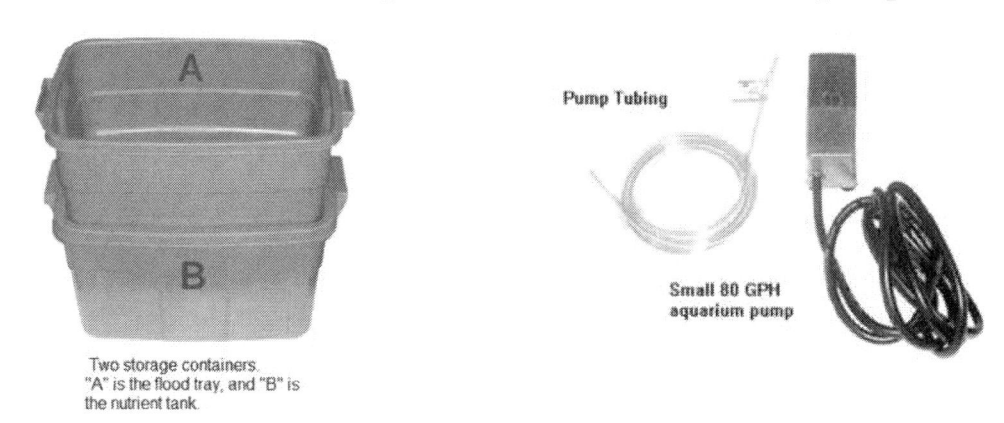

Two storage containers. "A" is the flood tray, and "B" is the nutrient tank.

Pieces and Parts

In addition to the containers and pump you will need a plastic matrix for the bottom of the flood tray, four flood pots and flood and drain fixtures. In the graphic, "A" is the flood fixture, "B" is the 1 1/4 " hole cutter and "C" is the drain fixture.

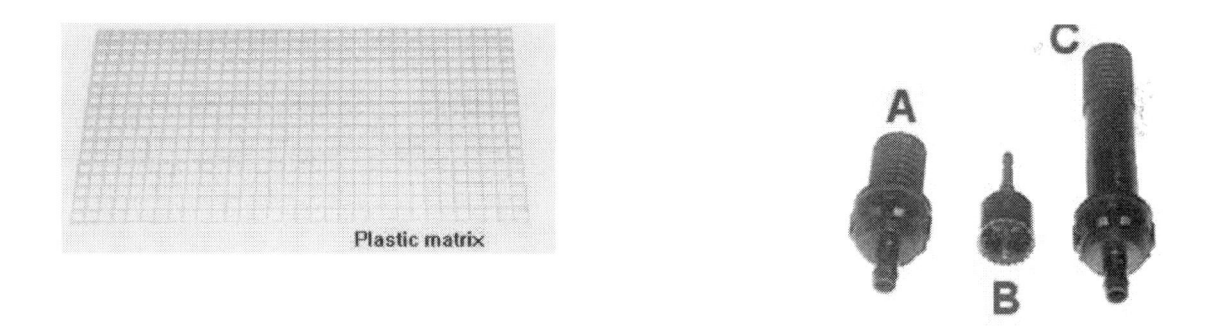

Plastic matrix

Construction

This step adds holes to the nutrient tank cover. The holes are cut so that when the upper flood tray (container) is placed on top of the nutrient tank cover the bottom of the flood and drain fixtures protrude into the nutrient tank. In the graphic, a 2" hole cutter was used.

To obtain accurate hole placement take the top container (before the flood and drain fixtures are installed) and set it on the nutrient tank lid and mark the center of the holes on the nutrient tank cover with a pen.

The plastic matrix is a plastic light fixture cover available at most home improvement centers. You will have to cut out a piece to fit your flood tank (tray). Note in the graphic that holes were cut out so the matrix will fit over the flood and drain fixtures. The matrix should fit flat on the bottom of the container.

View from the bottom of the 10 gallon container

Construction

In the graphic, you can see the flood and drain fixtures protruding through the bottom of the nutrient tank lid. Also note that the overflow fixture does not have any tubing. This is done on purpose so that the overflow will splash back into the nutrient tank and in the process, adding oxygen to the nutrient. A small hole was cut on the side of the nutrient tank so that the power cord can exit the tank.

Operation

Grow Rocks work very well in this sort of system. You can grow just about any type of plant you desire. Before you use the system, you should wash the grow rocks with water to remove any fine material left over from the kiln process. When you are ready to transplant flush the grow rocks with nutrient before placing the plant into the flood pots. Do this in the cool of the evening to reduce transplant shock. Your watering times will vary depending on the time of the year and the type and size of your plants. You might want to start out watering every two or three hours and observe your plants. If your plants are wilting they are not getting enough fluid. This time will decrease as the season gets hotter and you may have to water every hour or so. Set the flood time so that the nutrient level reaches the top of the overflow fixture. In the Author's system this took around 20 minutes to reach this level. Total flood time was set to 30 minutes. Good Luck with your ebb and flow system/

Ebb and flow trays can get really large as shown by the one shown below. These trays are also used to water pot plants.

Aeriation system

Aeriation Systems are also called bubbler systems.

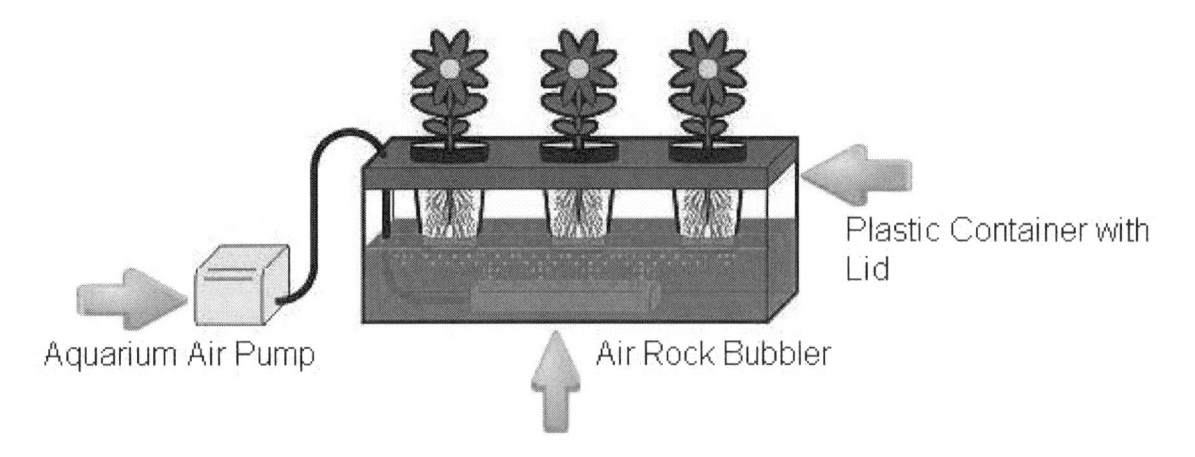

The aeration system is very simple to build and use. The system is composed of a simple plastic nutrient tank made from a plastic container with a lid and a small aquarium air pump to bubble oxygen to the roots of plants immersed in the nutrient solution. Plants are suspended above the solution by a small cup or pot that is inserted into holes cut in the container lid. The plant roots are submerged in the tank's nutrient solution. A layer of inert material, such as gravel, clay pebbles or vermiculite is placed in the pots or cups to provide stability for the plants while allowing the roots to grow down into the nutrient solution.

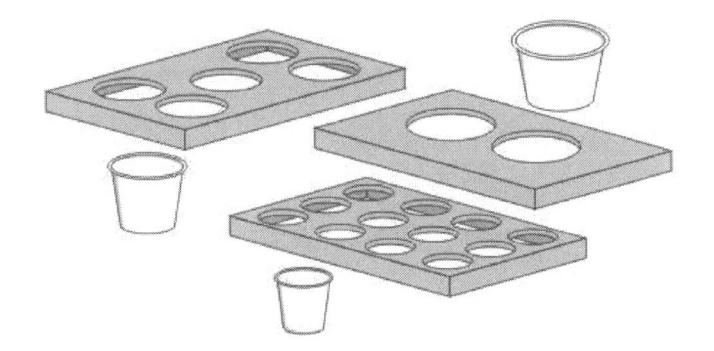

Bubbler top cover with various hole sizes for different size plants or cups.

The main advantage of the aeration system is simplicity.

The Bubble Machine

The Bubble Machine is a very simple but productive hydroponics system. The system consists of a plastic storage container with a lid. Holes are cut in the lid to receive plastic pots. An inexpensive air pump and bubble rock make up the rest of the system. A small plastic reducer is inserted in the side of the container and a piece of clear aquarium air pump tubing is used to gage the nutrient level. The number and size of the holes that are drilled in the lid depends on the plant and pot size. A large plant might just have one hole in the middle of the lid. The author's system has 5 holes and uses 4 inch pots. I drilled holes in the pots so the roots could grow through then and into the nutrient. This is a very trouble free system. This is the first hydroponics system I built and has remained my favorite.

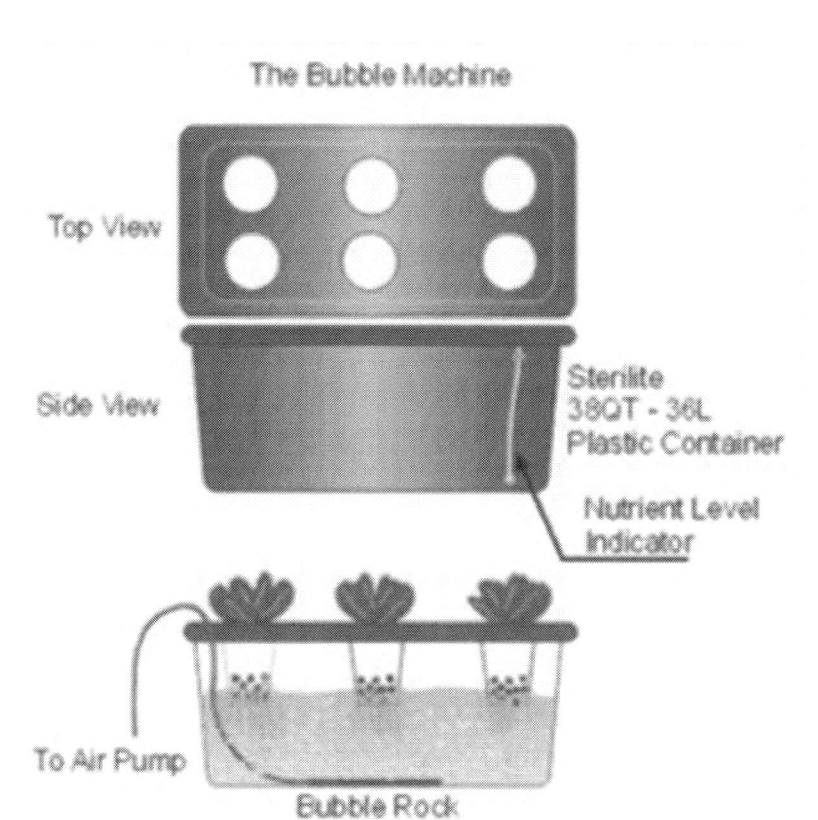

The nice thing about this system is that I can grow a spring crop of lettuce in the system before I dump the nutrient, and start over. This may not be possible with slower growing plants, or later in the warmer days of spring, as the plants will use more water. All you need to do is to add pH adjusted water until you have replaced the same volume of nutrient you started with. In my system, I started out with seeds placed in perlite and watered. After the seeds sprouted, I fed the plants a 50% nutrient solution. I then waited until the plants had true leaves, and were about 1-1/2 inch tall before moving them into the 4" pots that had been whetted with nutrient. I filled the nutrient tank until it over lapped the pots by about 1/2 ". I did this because the new plants did not have long roots and I wanted to be sure that the perlite in the pots came in contact with the nutrient.

The nice thing about this system is that I can grow a spring crop of lettuce in the system before I dump the nutrient, and start over. This may not be possible with slower growing plants, or later in the warmer days of spring, as the plants will use more water. All you need to do is to add pH adjusted water until you have replaced the same volume of nutrient you started with. In my system, I started out with seeds placed in perlite and watered. After the seeds sprouted, I fed the plants a 50% nutrient solution. I then waited until the plants had true leaves, and was about 1-1/2 inch tall before moving them into the 4" pots that had been whetted with nutrient. I filled the nutrient tank until it over lapped the pots by about 1/2 ". I did this because the new plants did not have long roots and I wanted to be sure that the perlite in the pots came in contact with the nutrient.

Remember that if you are starting this system a little late, you can go to your local nursery or home center and get your plants. If the plants you purchase are in a peat / soil mixture make sure to wash the roots before putting them in the media. I used perlite as a system medium, but "Grow Rocks" would work just as well. What can you grow in this type of system? Things like lettuce and herbs do quite well. You could grow other plants like green beans, squash and peppers. One squash plant would probably cover the entire system because of its large leaves. Make sure you think about how large a mature plant will be before adding a bunch of plants that later will compete for their place in the sun. If you want a trouble free system and want to enjoy successful hydroponics growing the first time out, then the Bubble Machine is it.

Results

The above was taken in late December in my new hobby greenhouse. I have already enjoyed a good salad from this system. The bubbler system is 5 years old and going strong. Once a year you will need to clean up the unit because of all the nutrient salt buildup.

The 1 Gallon Bubbler System

This bubbler system is a good example of making a hydroponics system from most anything. This system is constructed from 1 gallon plastic jugs. Two of them are milk jugs and the other one is from a distilled water jug that my wife used. Because you can see through the jugs, I painted them green with spray paint that is especially manufactured to paint plastic. When cutting off the tops, go slow, as the plastic is rather thin and easy to cut. If you are not careful, you will quickly cut the hole too big for the 2 inch net pots. Also, be careful not to wrinkle the plastic as you will create a crack. Because the plastic is so thin, they will probably only last one season. This system is a good project for school or for just having fun. Note that the end of the air tubing is connected to a small bubbler rock.

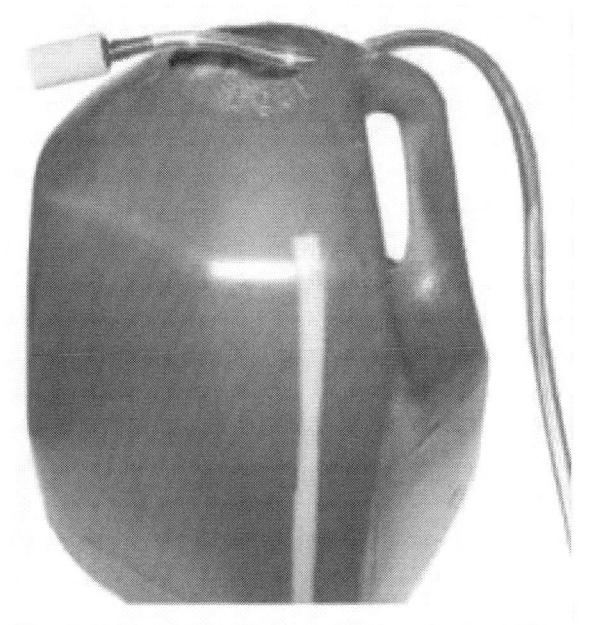

Painted 1 gallon milk jug with top removed for net cup. Note small bubbler rock.

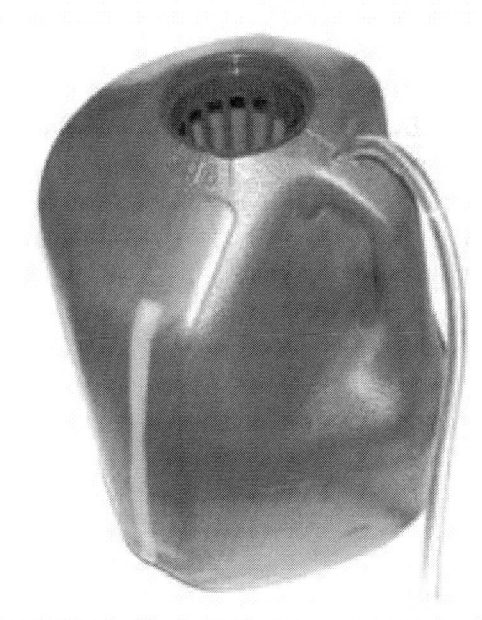

Finished jug. Note nutrient level window on side of jug.

The graphic above are of the completed 1 gallon bubbler. The air rock (stone) is placed at the bottom of the jug. Also note that when I painted the jug, I put some tape on the side of the jug so that when I removed it, I would have a small window (nutrient level window) on its side. Using this window, I can monitor the nutrient level of the jug. For this system, I made three of them and ran the bubblers from one air pump. If you have a lot of jugs and a lot of air pumps, there is probably no limit to how many of these could be made and put into operation.

Just as I had finished building the 1 gallon bubblers, my wife asked me if I could grow parsley for her as we were expecting a freeze and when that happens all her parsley is destroyed. The graphic on the left shows the parsley that eventually grew from small starts pulled from her garden and placed in the system. Note in the graphic that I have used LECA rock to hold the parsley plants she pulled out of her garden. I am thinking that if I had about 10 or 15 of these systems that I could grow almost all the herbs I would ever need.

Aeroponic Systems

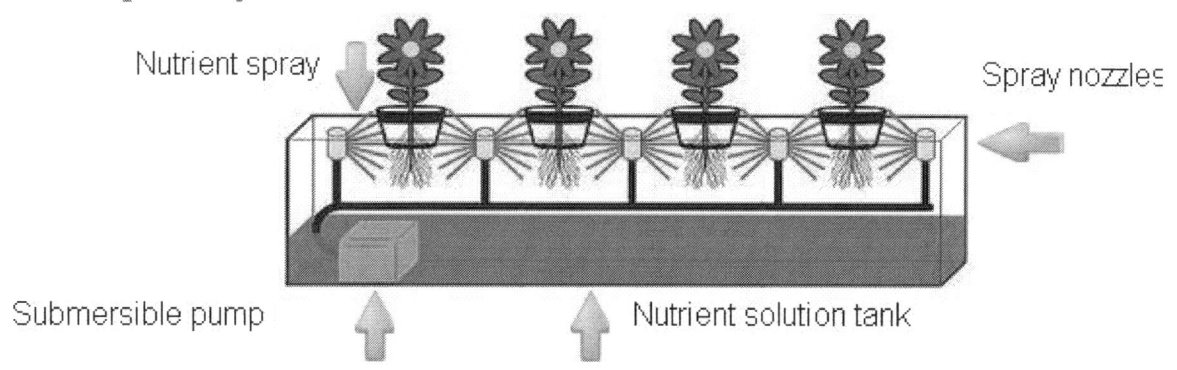

The Aeroponic System is more advanced than other types of the hydroponics systems. It is similar to the NFT system in that nutrients are supplied to the roots of a plant; but different in that it is supplied through a fine mist. In this system, the roots remain suspended and immersed in a culture or growing chamber, where they are sprayed with a mist of nutrient solution at short intervals. The nutrient solution is taken from a nutrient solution tank by a pump which feeds the mister nozzles or foggers. A timer programmed for very short irrigating cycles controls the pump. Like the NFT system, if the pump fails or there is a power interruption the plants' roots will dry quickly and result in plant loss. The liquid fed to the misters or foggers must be filtered, as they can quickly be clogged which could affect their performance. The Aeroponics System can cause fantastic growth rates of plants when it is done right. These systems are great for plant cloning.

Aeroponic Advantages & Disadvantages

The main advantage of the Aeroponic System is rapid growth and maximum production of plants grown using this technique. The system is simple in that there is no medium and the system only requires a timer, pump, and misters. The reason for the rapid growth is the plant gets exactly what it needs for maximum sustained growth. While other systems can do this, none approach the fine degree of control in this type of system.

Some of the disadvantages of the Aeroponic System is that it is only good for fast growing plants. To work properly the system must be setup properly and great attention must be given to the timing and amount of nutrient that is used. As stated, this system works really well when used for cloning plants.

If you have made a trip to Disney World in Florida, you have probably seen their Aeroponic System.

Mister Cloner

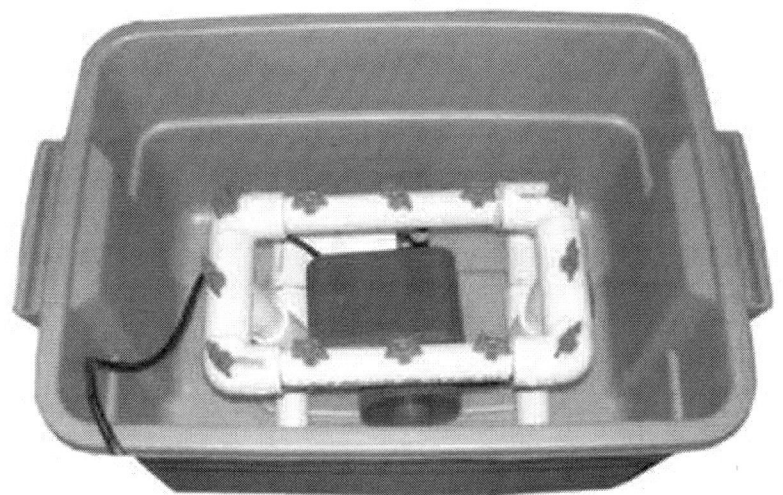

How can you create a plant without a seed? A clone is a cutting taken from another plant, often called a mother plant and then rooted. A clone will have every quality of the mother plant including sex, hardiness, diseases and stresses. This section shows an example of a mister cloner as shown above. The cloner uses a little PVC pipe, some landscape misters, a plastic container, a submersible pump and a few net pots. This project could easily be done in one evening.

Parts List

Your mister cloner may be a bit different from the one described depending if you can obtain the Rubbermaid container. The actual size is not that important but how one is constructed. Most of the parts except for the pump and net pots can be found at a local home improvement store. There is a huge numbers of videos on the web describing this type of mister cloner.

1 - Rubbermaid 3 gallon (11.3L) container. 16 x 10.7 x 7 in. Rubbermaid calls the container "Roughneck"
12 - misters The ones I used are Full Circle Misters (Green color) and 165 degree (orange ones). Also available over the Internet and at hydroponics stores. You may just want to use all 165 degree models.
1 - Rio Submersible pump Rio-2500 which pumps 2972 LPH (772 GPH). Found at better pet stores or over the Internet and at hydroponics stores.
1 - 6 to 8 ft. section of 1" thin wall PVC pipe (or less) - Note all 1" parts are used.
4 - 90 degree elbows
4 - Tee fittings
3 - end plugs
1 - Threaded 90 degree elbow
1 - Threaded adaptor (screws into the above fitting)
1 - 1" threaded to 1/2 inch Irrigation line adaptor L-adaptor

10 - 2" net pots
1 -2" hole cutter
LECA or rockwool media

The first step is to decide how many net pots you want in in your cloner. In the example above, 10 holes were drilled with a 2" hole cutter. 2" nets pots fit perfectly in the cut out holes.

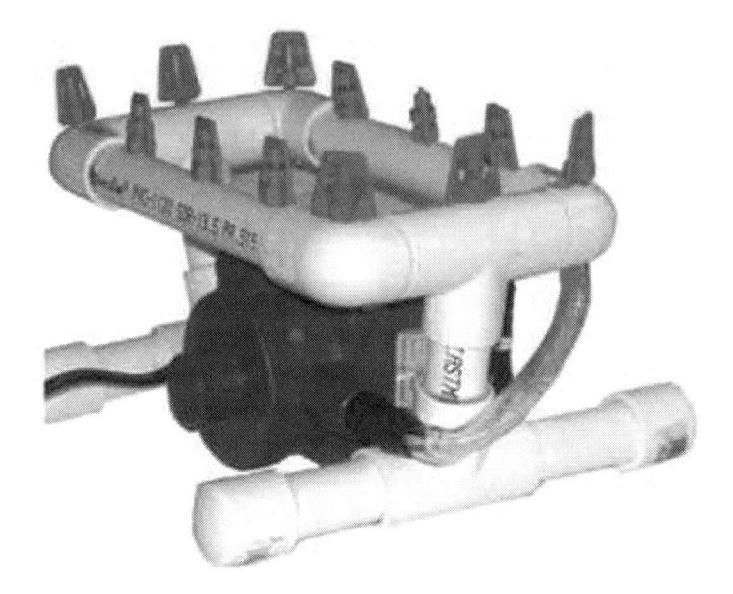

After finishing the net pot holder, it is time to construct the plumbing that holds the misters and receives nutrient from the Rio pump. The assembly I built has rectangular dimensions of approximately 8 1/2" by 4 3/4", and a 4" height. Make sure that after cutting the PVC, you de-burr everything and make sure there are no cuttings left.

Also, before gluing everything together drill holes for the misters as this will also cause cuttings to be left inside the PVC pipe. Keeping things very clean will prevent your misters from being plugged up.

To install the misters, drill 16/64" holes for each mister. Note that you may use other misters and this hole size may change. The misters I used are threaded and actually threat themselves into the drilled hole. No threading of the PVC pipe was required.

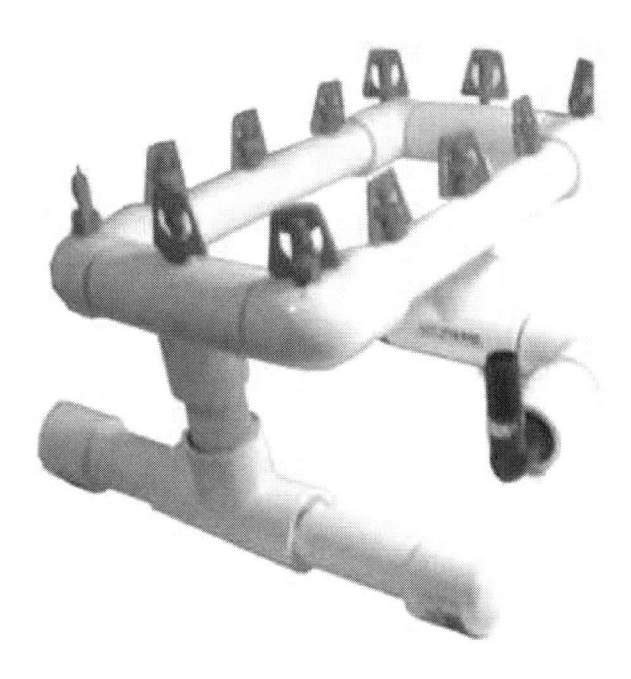

Note that on one side of the foot is the pump input connection. As stated in the parts, the 1" elbow is threaded on one end. Into these threads is screwed a threaded 1" to 1" adapter and into this adapter a 1" to 1/2 inch irrigation 90 degree elbow is attached. I only hand tightened all the threaded components with no leaks. Another option could be to drill and tap a connection directly into the PVC pipe and screw in an irrigation adapter.

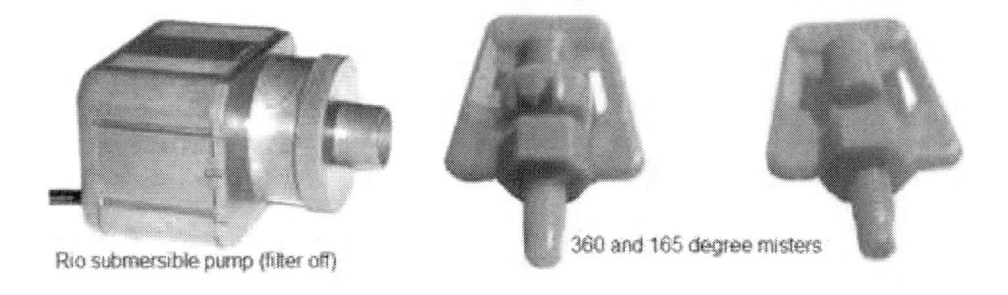

Rio submersible pump (filter off)

360 and 165 degree misters

The misters shown on the right are what I used. There are also other types of misters that would work just as well.

Misting takes a lot of power to move all the fluids used by the system and I finally ended up using the Rio 2500 which moves around 772 gallons per hour. Anything smaller will probably not work.

This is the system with the spray (mister) assembly in the Rubbermaid container. If you are using other sizes of containers for the cloner, you may have to determine the size of the spray unit. Just make sure that all the net pots receive spray from the misters.

Operational suggestions
The mister cloner will be operated 24/7. The net pots will receive the plant that you want to root. In reality, no media would be needed, as it will only be used to hold the plant while it grows roots. Because the pump must push nutrient through the small holes in the mister, I would suggest that only LECA or rockwool be used in the net pots. The LECA and rockwool do three things. First it protects the plant and its soon to be roots from sun light. Second, it holds the plant in the net pot. Third, it provides a wet humid environment for the cutting. The author enjoys cloning tomato plants by pulling the suckers from his plants. If the cloner is to be successful, you should keep things as clean as possible. You will need to check mister operation on a regular basis. If one is plugged, shut down the operation (be safe and remove power from the pump) and replace the plugged one with a fresh one. Plants will clone faster if the cutting is cut at a 45 degree angle and the part (end) of the plant that will be exposed to the nutrient be rough up (scraped).This exposes the inner part of the cutting. The nutrient used for cloning could be just tap water, but the author uses a 1/2 strength nutrient as the liquid. You will have to monitor the nutrient level from time-to-time, especially in the warmer months. Some pumps will not tolerate running dry (your plants surely won't) so make sure that you protect your plants and expensive pump. One last note and that is to run a couple of fresh changes (or more) of water through the system

before using it. The solvent used to connect the PCV pipe needs to be washed out before using.

Good luck with your cloner.

Commercial Systems

The commercial system on the right uses the same technique as the mister cloner above. That is that nutrient is pumped up and out of spray nozzles onto the plant roots. The nutrient then trickles down into the tank below and is reused on a continuous basis. This system is called a tower system and ideal for use where space may be at a premium. These systems are available as kits, or look on YouTube for some video on these systems.

The system below is a feature at the O'Hare Airport.

The system below is from and is a HydroCycle Vertical Aeroponic System

HydroCycle Vertical Aeroponic Systems utilize unique grow tubes that support the flow of oxygen for rapid growth and a nutrient-rich mist for healthy plants. Grow an unbelievable 220 plants in less than 23 square feet!

- These compact systems are ideal for growth in tight spaces and maximum control of the root zones.

- Aeroponics delivers a high-pressured mist that delivers nutrients to the root zone.

- The 10" tube diameter gives the root zone maximum aeration that helps the plants to grow quickly.

- Each system comes with an air pump with ceramic air diffusers, Y-fit snap hook tube hangers, all the necessary plumbing and fittings and more depending on the system that is purchased.

Drip systems

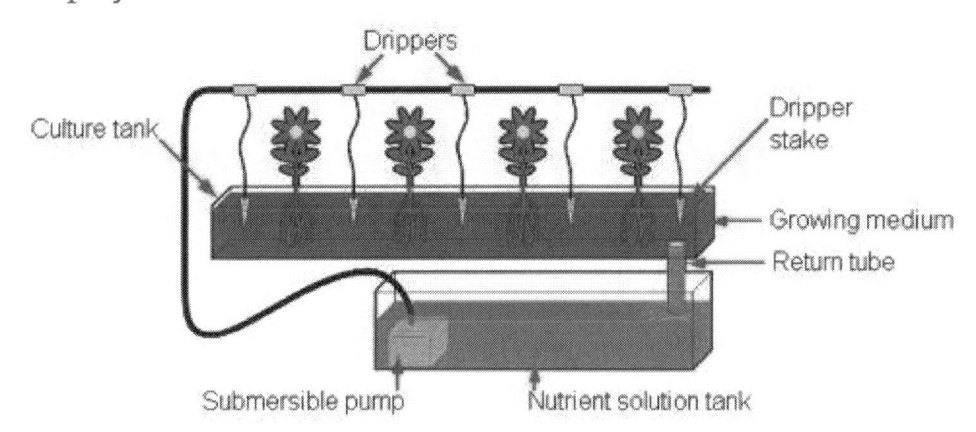

The drip system is probably the world's most common hydroponics system. The operation of a drip system is very simple. Nutrient is pumped out of a nutrient solution tank and fed to drippers which regulate the amount of fluid passing through it. The dripper is then connected to a dripper stake which is inserted in the growing medium next to the plant. In most hydroponics operations, the pump is cycled for a time and then cutoff. The nutrient then flows through the medium and back into the nutrient solution tank via a return tube which is attached to the culture tank. When the plants are small, the amount of time between watering is large. As the plant gets larger it will require shorter times between watering.

2 Box Dripper

Parmex carrots

When I decided that I wanted to grow hydroponics carrots, I decided that I wanted to use a drip system. The system would use growrocks (LECA) at the bottom and a mixture of perlite and coconut fiber for the actual medium that the carrots would grow in. I plan to grow Parmex carrots

The dripper system (above) is nothing more than 1 large Rubbermaid container used as the nutrient tank, and two smaller Rubbermaid containers that hold the media

Finished drip manifold.

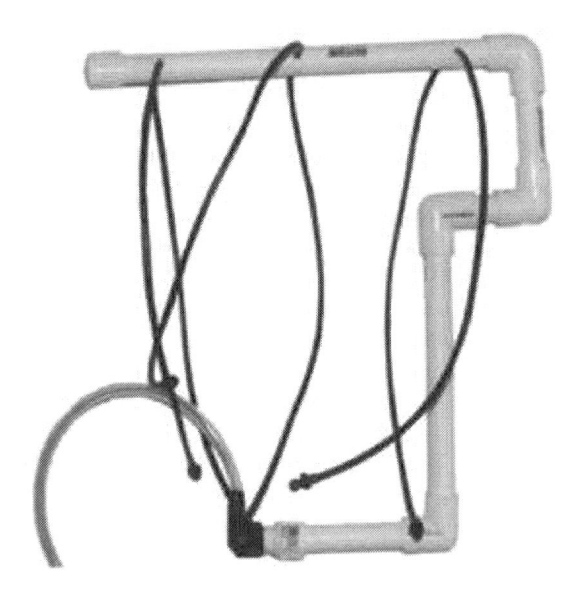

Note that irrigation drip tubing has goof plugs on the end.

Parts List
1 - Rubbermaid "Roughneck"
10 gallon 24 x 16 x 8 3/4 in. container
2 - Rubbermaid "Roughneck" 3 gallon 16 x 10.7 x 7 inch container
1 - 6 to 8 ft. section of 1" thin wall PVC pipe (or less) - All 1" parts are used.
1 - PT-2090 Exo Terra Repti-Flo 200 LPH
pump (52 gallons per hour)
4 - 90 degree elbows
1 - 5/8" grommet
1 - 1/2 inch irrigation "tee" (or L)
1 - 7" piece of 5/8 "blue" tubing
1 - Threaded fitting
1 - 1/2 inch irrigation connector (connects to above fitting) See above
1 - end plug
10 ft. irrigation drip tubing
6 - goof plugs
LECA, Perlite and coconut fiber media
Measurements (approx) from plug back to pump connection:
11 3/4", 3 1/2", 2", 8 1/2" and 4 1/2"

Because the top of the large plastic container (lid) is recessed, it is ideal as it will receive the top two smaller containers. Note that I have cut 5 drain holes to receive the nutrient as it drips through the system and back into the nutrient tank. This is done for both of the top media holders. Also note that I have used a 5/8 inch grommet and an irrigation "tee" along with some blue tubing to monitor nutrient level. The other side of the "tee" is used to drain the nutrient reservoir. If this is not needed, then use a 1/2" irrigation 'L" fitting.

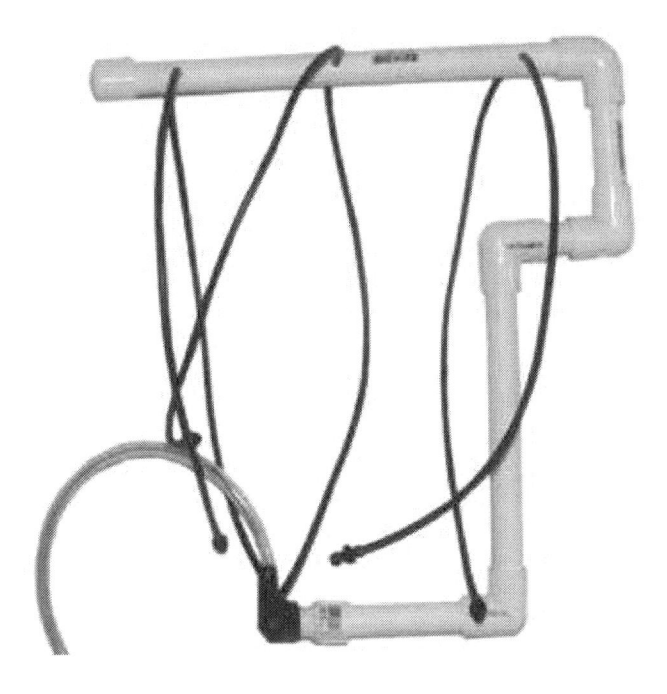

The drip manifold.is made from PVC tubing. Note that plastic drip line is inserted in the manifold in three places. I used a drill bit that was just a bit smaller than the drip tubing, so when forced into the hole it will be held in place. To close off the ends of the drip lines I used 6 goof plugs. Holes were then punched through 1 side of the drip tubing at about 1 inch intervals with a hot needle. Be very careful doing this as you could easily melt a large hole in the tubing. Also make sure that the first hole is not too close to the header and is over the medium container.

Tips on the manifold:
Make sure when you make all your cuts to be sure that all shavings and edges are smooth and free of burrs. Clean up each piece with water and make a visual inspection. This will insure that the manifold if free of debris and will not plug your drip lines.

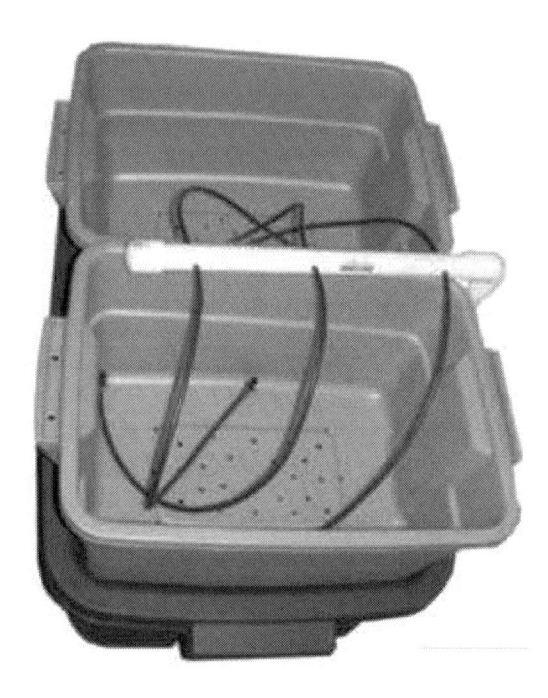

Once you have finished the construction, tie off the manifold with a tie wrap by drilling holes and running a cable tie wrap between the two medium containers and over the manifold. This will stabilize the drip manifold. Do this at two places.

Setting up
Place about 1 1/2 inch of LECA rocks in both of the media containers. Then mix a 70 / 30 mixture of coconut fiber and perlite. Fill both of the media containers with this mixture to about 1 1/2 inch from the top. What you do next is controlled by what you are going to grow. If you are going to transplant plants like lettuce, then you will need full strength nutrient. If you are going to start seeds in the system, then you will need to start the seeds as you normally would. In this manner, you would wet the medium

with water and then wait for germination.

Waiting on the seeds to germinate.

Carrot sprouts in coconut fiber and perlite.

Getting Started:

As I said earlier, I wanted to grow carrots in my system. Starting the carrot seeds is no different than any other operation. In the graphic above, The drip system is not installed, and I will wait until the seeds have their first real leaves before I start dripping. After waiting for about 5 days my wait was rewarded by some carrot sprouts as shown on the right.

Carrots the author pulled a bit early. The Parmex carrots are very sweet.

After the seeds have germinated and developed some leaves, you might start with a 1/2 half strength nutrient for a few days. At that point, you could drain the nutrient and replace it with full strength.

Drip times

You will need a timer to turn on and off the nutrient pump. You might start with an application of nutrient once a day for 15 minutes and off at night. The number of cycles will all depend on the growth state of the plants and the temperature. As days get longer and plants get larger, they will need more nutrient.

Good Results

Dip Stick Special

The Dip Stick Special is a very popular type of system. Many people have published plans for this type of system. The following is the author's version. This system is a drip system that is powered by an air pump. The system is constructed out of plastic buckets, one sitting in the other. The top container holds the growing medium and the bottom holds the nutrient.

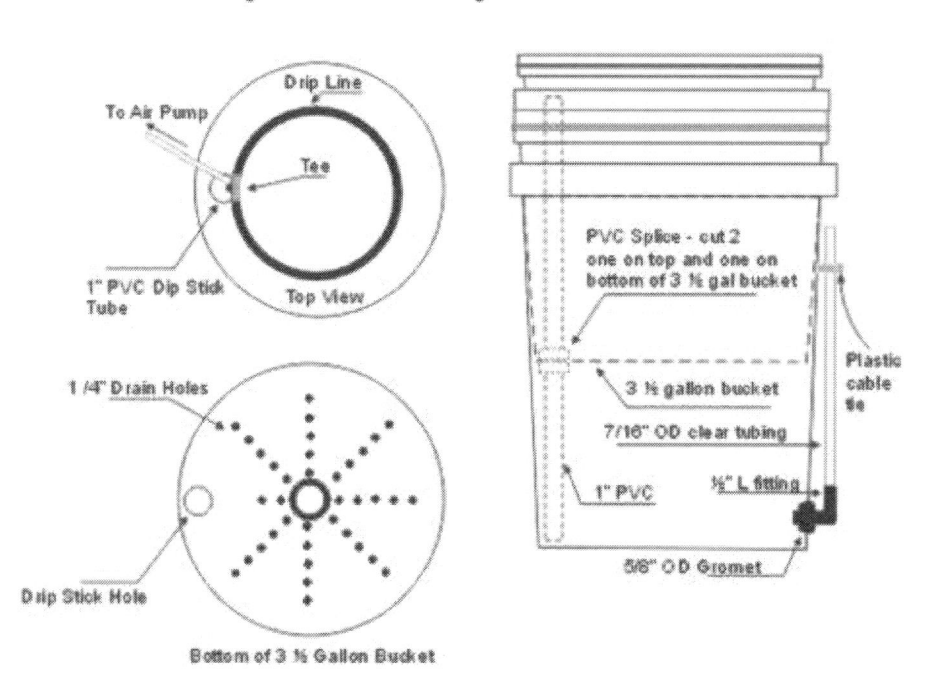

The top bucket has holes drilled in its bottom so nutrient can flow into the lower nutrient tank. A 1" PVC pipe is placed through a hole in the top container and held in place by two pieces cut from a PVC splice and glued with PVC cement on each side of the bottom of the bucket. Tubing from the air pump and from the drip line are passed through this pipe.

The drip loop is constructed around a 1/2" irrigation tee fitting. I found that that a small piece of 7/16" clear tubing with in ID of 5/16" could be shoved into the tee. Its a tight fit, but works fine. The drip loop is constructed out of 3/8" mist tubing. This is inserted into the clear 7/16" tubing which is already inserted in the tee. Again the fit is very close, but gives a nice snug fit. The loop on the Author's system is about 8" in diameter. Yours may be larger or smaller depending on the size of your bucket. On the other part of the tee, I used more of the clear 7/16" tubing. This passes through the 1" PVC dip stick pipe and goes into the bottom of the nutrient tank. My nutrient bucket came from a local fast food burger store for free and was used to hold sliced pickles. I had to purchase the 3 1/2 gallon medium bucket, because these are not as common as the 5 gallon. If you do not want to beg buckets, you can purchase them. In the case of the pickle bucket, I filled it up with a bleach and water solution. This cleaned the bucket and removed the pickle smell. The nutrient bucket construction is rather simple. Drill a 3/4" hole in the side of the bucket near the bottom. This hole will take a 5/8" grommet. Through this grommet, connect a 1/2" irrigation L connector. Then insert a piece of the 7/16" clear tubing into the L. This tubing, which is run up the side of the 5 gallon bucket will become the nutrient gage. Cut two holes at the top of the bucket, and use a plastic cable tie to secure the gage

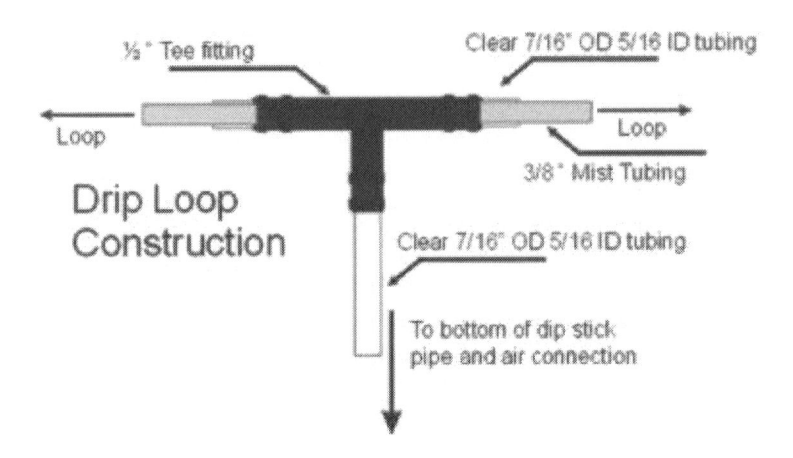

Construction of the lower part of the drip system is rather simple. First construct your drip loop. Next you will drill holes on the side of the 1" pipe near the bottom (see below). Insert the tubing from the drip loop and the air pump through the dip stick and feed both of them out the holes. Make sure that the drip loop ring is flat against the dip stick top. Then cut the drip loop tubing, leaving about 1-1/2" of tubing from the side of the dip stick. Drill a 13/64" hole in the bottom of the "L" fitting.

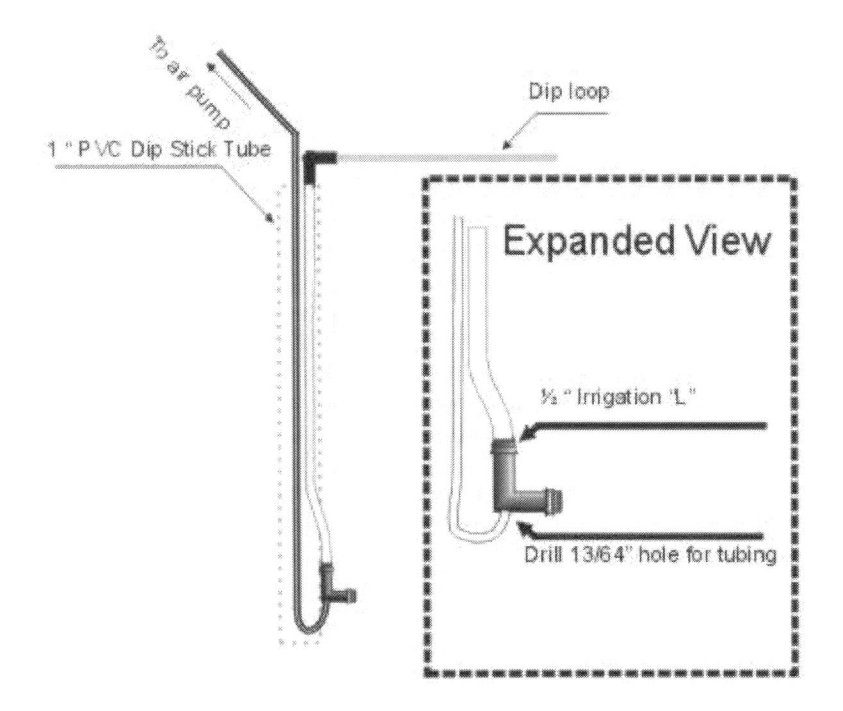

Then insert the air line tubing into this hole. This will be a snug fit. Then insert the large tubing into the top of the irrigation "L". Again this will be a very snug fit. When finished, use a tie wrap to hold the "L" on the 1" PVC pipe. Make sure that there are no kinks in the air line tubing.

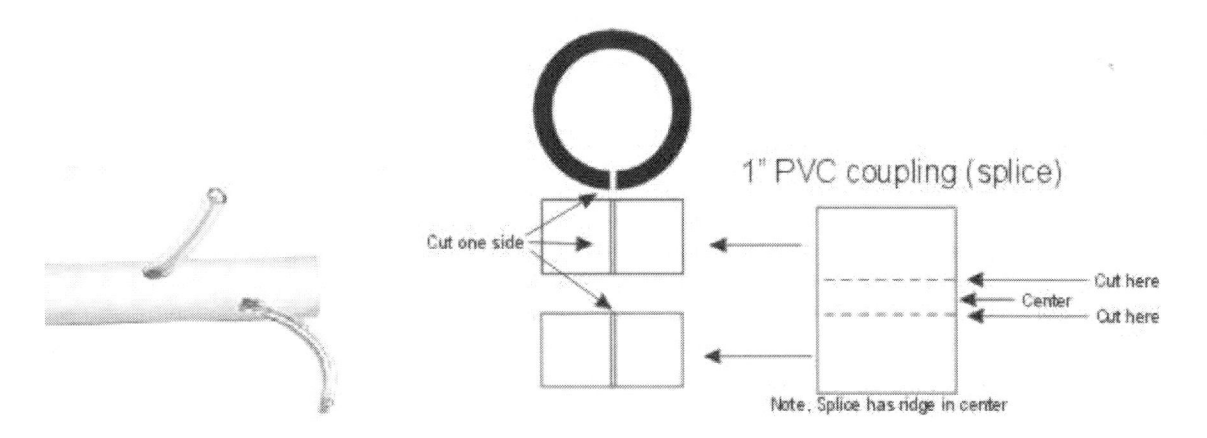

After you have constructed all the parts, then you are ready to set up the system. Here are a few suggestions:

If you are going to grow a large plant like a tomato, get a larger air pump. Most pet stores or hydroponics shops have these heavier air pumps. The more air, the faster the drip. Note that the air pushes the nutrient up the air line.

The next step is to add the medium. You should use 100% "Grow Rocks". From experience, I know that the "Grow Rocks" work very well. If you are using "Grow Rocks" make sure you have washed them very well, because any loose material could clog up the system.

Next, place the medium bucket into the nutrient bucket and add the nutrient to a level just below the medium bucket bottom. Flush the nutrient through the medium and into the bucket below. This will wet the medium.

After this is done, you are ready to add your plant(s). It is suggested that you be careful what you use to grow your plants in before transplanting. If they were grown in peat or soil, you might want to wash them very well before transplanting. This will remove matter that could plug up the system. After starting the system, monitor the nutrient level every day and add back pH adjusted water into the system as needed. When you have replaced the same volume of nutrients you started with it is time to dump the nutrient and start over with fresh. What can you grow in the Dip Stick Special? I would think that if it has roots, then you could grow it. plants like lettuce, tomatoes, peppers, green beans, herbs of all types and even banana trees do well!

Head and nutrient line
4' - 3/8" Mist tubing (for drip head - see note)
1 - 1/2" black plastic irrigation "tee" connector
1 - 1/2" black plastic irrigation "L" connector
3' - 1" white PVC pipe
1 - 1" white PVC splice (Note, cut into two pieces, and cut on one side so it will slip over 1" pipe.
1 - 5/8" grommet (to receive "L" and gage tubing)
3-1/2 gallons "Grow Rocks"
1 - can PVC cement
2 - Plastic cable ties

Note: the mist tubing was found at a Lowe's Home Center, and is used in a mist system. Made by a company called Arizona Mist.

Note, General Hydroponics makes a drip head kit (GH FARM KIT Item # 4115). This can be purchased from many hydroponics dealers that sell General Hydroponics equipment and supplies. If you purchase the kit, then all you will need is the buckets, "Grow Rocks" and the air pump.

I buffed up the white lower bucket with sand paper and painted it green.

General Hydroponics Drip Kit

Note how the splice on the top and bottom of the bucket keep the "Dip Stick" in place.

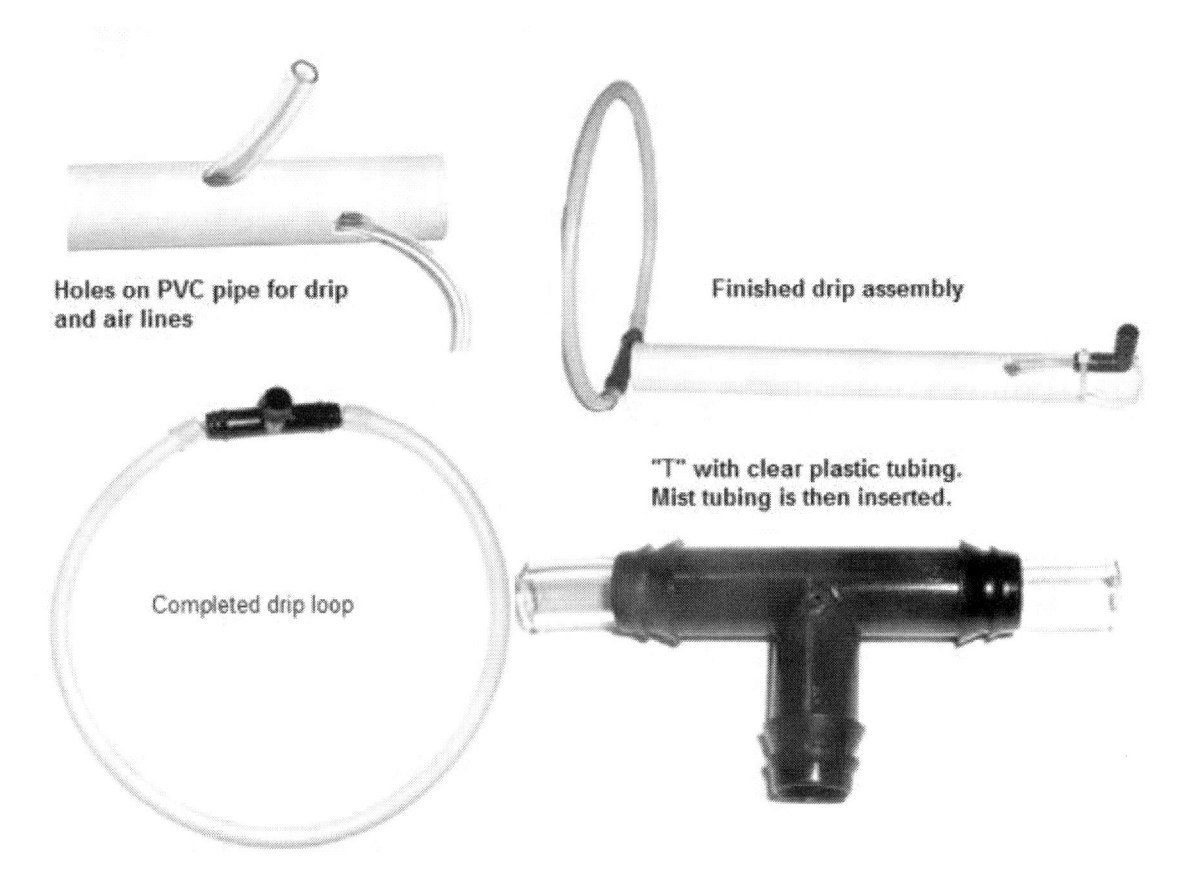

Holes on PVC pipe for drip and air lines

Finished drip assembly

Completed drip loop

"T" with clear plastic tubing. Mist tubing is then inserted.

Comments and suggestions

The Dip Stick Special is a great system to start with as it is simple and easy to construct. You can also purchase this system commercially if you wish. I would suggest that you use grow rocks in this system or have some way of regulating the drip rate if you use media that retains moisture longer than grow rocks. A problem that I ran into with this system was the clear plastic used for the fluid gage on the side of the buckets. This tends to allow algae to grow inside the tube. A better answer may to purchase some of the blue plastic tubing sold by General Hydroponics. This tubing will fit over the 1/2 inch irrigation "L", and limit the sunlight that is causing algae growth. As the season gets warmer you will have to add water on a regular basis. Not only will the plant use a lot of water, but evaporation will use a lot as well. Never let the nutrient level get low, as the system does not pump as well with lower than normal fluid levels. Try and keep the level just below the bottom of the top bucket or net pot. Using a net pot in this system makes construction very easy, and I have purchased these pots for less than $3.00. Good Luck with your system.

Aquaponics System

Aquaponics What Is It?

Aquaponics is a system that combines conventional aquaculture (raising things like fish) with hydroponics in a symbiotic environment. Or growing food using fish poo! Well not exactly. The excreted fish solids are normally captured in a filter (Biofilter). In an aquaponics system, water from the fish is then fed into a hydroponic system where the by-products are broken down by bacteria into nitrites. The nitrates are utilized by the plants in the hydroponic system as nutrients.

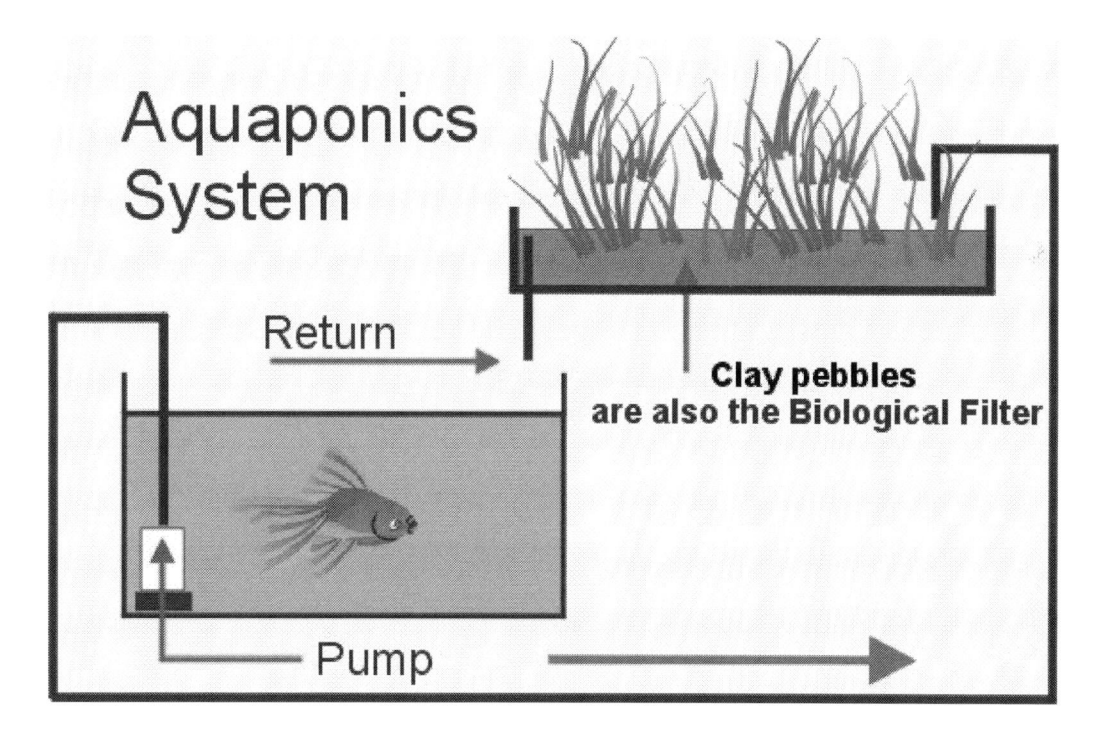

In the simplified system above, the clay pebbles are the Bio Filter. While this works, the pebbles have to be dumped and cleaned from time to time. The best solution is to use a vortex filter as shown below.

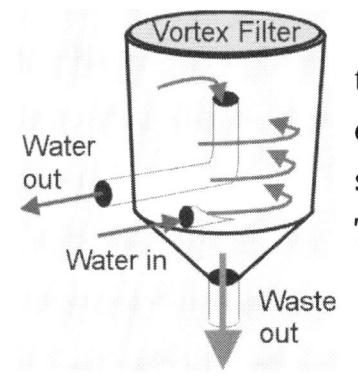

Water from the fish grow tank is pumped into the filter at the bottom. This causes a swirling current in the filter. Solids drop out to the bottom of the filter and clean nutrient water is sucked down the water outlet which is higher than the input. This is then fed to where it is needed. The waste out would have a valve on the outlet and could be drained. The solids make wonderful fertilizer.

While I don't have any plans for an Aquaponics system, I do like how they work and there is something rather soothing about fish. The one problem I see is this type of system while it works just fine as a small system, but a really large system would require a lot of power and is not all that practical for someone trying to grow food during the SGSM. While there are some really large Aquaponics systems out there, I don't think that as a commercial venture few have been successful. Most just look like some of the graphics I have inserted below. If you like what you see, then try one. They are actually pretty simple.

The above graphic - Attribution-Share Alike 2.0 Generic license.

Note added to the above graphic: Aquaponics: there are catfish in this tank, feeding the plants above, which feed the worms below, which feed the catfish.

The above graphic is licensed under the Creative Commons Attribution 3.0 Unported license.

Note added to the graphic: The raft tank at the Crop Diversification Centre (CDC) South Aquaponics greenhouse in Brooks, Alberta.

Float and Raft Systems

This is one system I like but I don't see this being something being used in a house unless it is a small one.

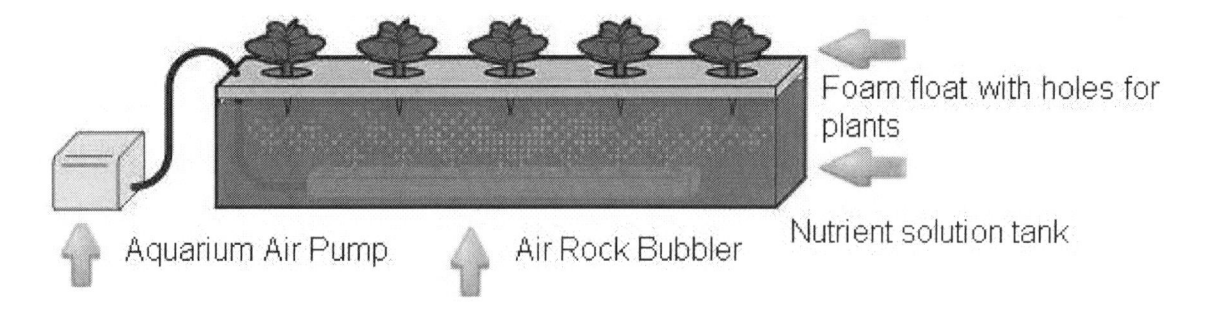

Another simple system is the floating bed or raft system. In this system, the plants are anchored in a floating platform made of Styrofoam and placed directly on the surface of the nutrient solution which is contained in a tank. The exposed roots of the plant are completely submerged in this solution. Oxygen is added to the solution by bubbling air from an air pump. Larger raft systems also recirculated the nutrient while adding oxygen. Huge amounts of lettuce can be grown with this type of system. This system is generally used for small plants that need very large quantities of water as in the case of lettuce. It would be possible with this sort of system to produce lettuce all year long if placed indoors and artificial light is provided.

Advantages and disadvantages of Floating Bed or Raft System

The main advantage of the float / raft system is that the plant roots are always exposed to adequate supplies of water, oxygen and nutrients. It is also a simple type of system to build and uses inexpensive materials. Another advantage is that leafy vegetables like lettuce and herbs thrive in this system.

Some of the disadvantages of the float / raft system are that it cannot be used to grow long term plants like tomatoes, and is heavy because all the liquid nutrients are put in a large container or tank. As you know, water is very heavy. This type of system could not easily be moved around.

Why would the home grower want to use a Float Bed or Raft System?

This type of system is pretty simple to build. Many people have tried this type of system by using a child's plastic swimming pool in the back yard. The system is low maintenance as it only uses a simple air pump to bubble oxygen into the nutrient. I have seen herbs, lettuce and pole beans grown in this simple system. You might want to consider building one of these systems as your first system. Styrofoam is available from most home centers and swimming pools are available at most large grocery stores and of course at Wall-Mart! Another way to make this type of system is to construct the nutrient chamber out of wood, and line it with thick plastic. The float system is a proven winner for producing herbs and lettuce and it will probably work for you as well.

Soda-Pop Special

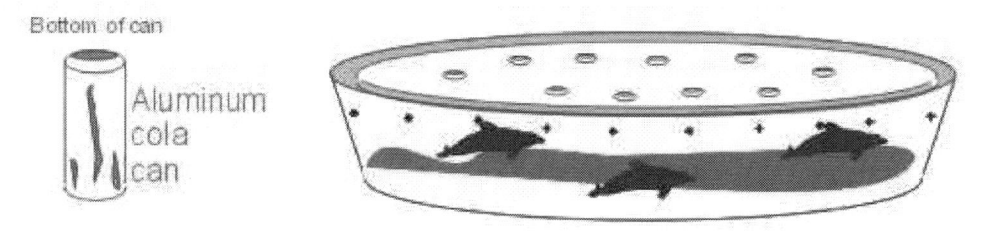

The "Soda Pop Special" is a static, non-circulating system that uses no electricity. You can grow just about anything you want with this system, but some longer maturing plants like tomatoes and peppers will take a little more time and attention. My Grand-daughter could not understand why I wanted to drill holes in her plastic swimming pool, but it became okay after I told her I would purchase her another one! This system uses a child's swimming pool. A circular piece of builders foam is cut out to fit inside of the pool.

Building this system is a good way to recycle all those aluminum cola cans. Using a hand operated can opener, cut out the bottom of the soda can. Cut the circular ridge that runs around the bottom. This part of the can will become the top of the medium holder. Make sure that you keep the opening tab inside of the can. Move the tab close to the opening, so that the coconut medium will not fall out. We will talk about the soda cans later.

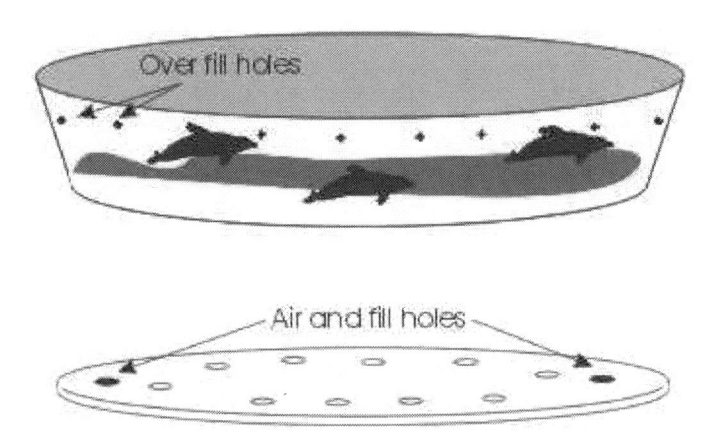

Over fill holes

Air and fill holes

Start building the system by cutting out a circular piece of builders foam. This foam is blue in color and has a plastic seal on both sides. Cut the foam so it will fit down into the pool and only have about 1/4 inch or less of space between the pool and the foam. Next drill holes around the pool about 3 inches up from the bottom. This will vary on the pool size. The point to be made here is that the holes must be below the circular foam piece. On the circular foam cut holes that will friction fit the aluminum soda cans. How many you cut will depend on the plants you might grow. A good suggestion is to grow pole beans on the back section of the pool and lettuce and basil in the front.

Air and fill holes

Aluminum cola cans

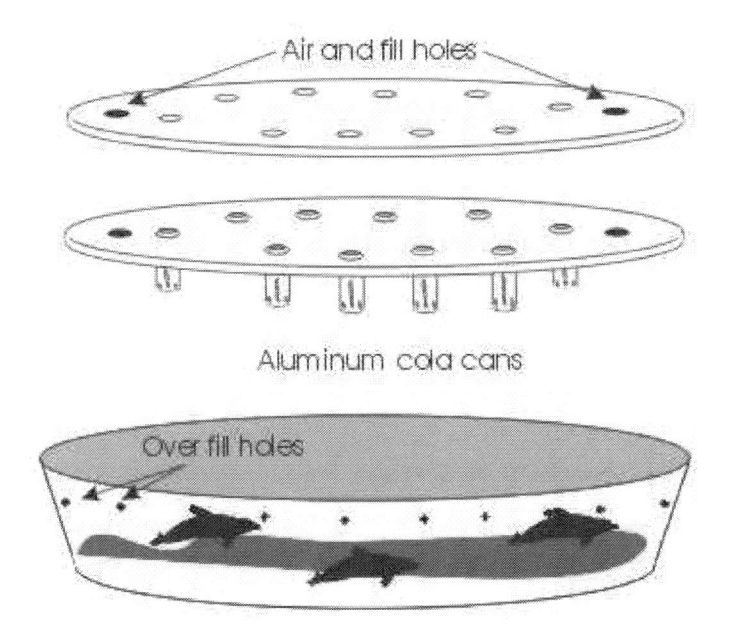

Over fill holes

The next step is to place the circular piece of foam into the pool. I used builders bricks in the bottom of the pool to hold up the foam. Make sure that you have a nutrient and air hole on opposite sides of the foam piece. Once the foam is in the pool, fill it with nutrient until it starts leaking out holes drilled in the sides of the pool. Next, take the aluminum cans with the bottoms removed and fill them with coconut fiber. Make sure that you tap the can on a hard surface to remove any air space in the can. Using a sharp knife, cut two slits down the can on opposite sides. This will provide space for roots to exit the can. Place the cans in the holes in the foam and wait for about 30 minutes, or until the coconut fiber wicks up the nutrient. When this happens, place your seeds into the cans. Beans about 1 inches deep, and lettuce and basil 1/4 inch

Monitor the nutrient level as the plants grow. When adding nutrient add it in both holes cut for this purpose as this will mix the fresh nutrient better. Sit back and enjoy your new low energy garden!

Parts List
1 - Child's plastic swimming pool
1 - Sheet of builders foam
6 to 10 aluminum soda cans
1 - Brick of coconut fiber

5 – Builders bricks

Finished System

Once you seeds germinate, continue to monitor the nutrient level. As the level drops, add more nutrient. If you are growing lettuce you will probably never have to add any nutrient. If you are growing beans, tomatoes or cucumbers you will have to add nutrient as it is used. If you are careful with pH, and EC, you can get by with just adding nutrient as this type of system does not have the high EC and pH fluctuations as powered systems do.

Commercial Float Systems

The picture below is the Growers Supply **HydroCycle Raft Beds. Below is a good example of what can be done with the Float and Raft Systems.**

The HydroCycle Raft Bed creates a beneficial environment for leafy greens. Easily produce kale, swiss chard, herbs, lettuce and more on a year-round basis.

These systems suspend roots in nutrient-rich water. This allows growers to fine-tune the solution to their plants' precise needs, ensuring the finest harvests.

Maximize production, without overcrowding crops. Growers are able to layout the raft bed to best suit their needs. Plant sites can be arranged to provide plants with the perfect amount of space.

Durable raft is made to last in any growing environment. The frame is constructed from 16-gauge, square steel pipe. The rafts are made from 1-1/2" Styrofoam, which also provides insulation. The bed is lined with 24 mil PolyMax®.

Non Electrical Systems

There are also a huge numbers of food growing systems that don't need electrical power. Usually the electricity is used to operate some sort of a pump that delivers nutrients to the plants or air to the plant roots, but non electrical systems only use human and sun power to grow food. Below are some of these systems

- Grow Bags
- Karatky type systems
- And of course a regular soil type gardens

Grow Bags

Weed-less growing – Ya Baby!

WHAT CAN YOU GROW IN A GROW BAG?

© Surviving the Super Grand Solar Minimum 2019

Shop Here at this URL

- High quality nonwoven fabric, better than plastic container, protect environment

- Decreased risk of transplant shock with bag handles

- Keeps plant warmer in winter and cooler in the summer, Allow the root breathe, Prevents roots circling and air-prunes plant's root structure

- Package: 5-pack 7 gallon grow bags

- Promise: The quality and service is our first aim. we can refund if you do not like our product

- Black Interior and White Exterior for superior performance, reflecting light back towards your garden
- Thick durable construction
- Low cost alternative to plastic nursery or ceramic pots
- Used by commercial greenhouse growers for drip irrigation or top feed applications
- When filled with media bags easily stand upright

Shop Here at this URL Many different sizes available.

The answer is:

PRETTY WELL ALMOST ANYTHING

How I did it:

Grow Bags are Plastic and heavy heavy-duty felt reusable which are economical and easy to use. You can fill them with soil or other mixes. The plastic bags have pre-punched holes to allow for good water drainage.

This is the Authors greenhouse filled with black plastic grow bags. The bags are watered with a drip system. **Note, if you don't have a way to use a drip system, you can quite easily just hand water and fertilize.**

Purple Peppers on the left of the path and three types of eggplant on the right - Then the Tomatoes and then on the far right of the High Tunnel are my cucumbers

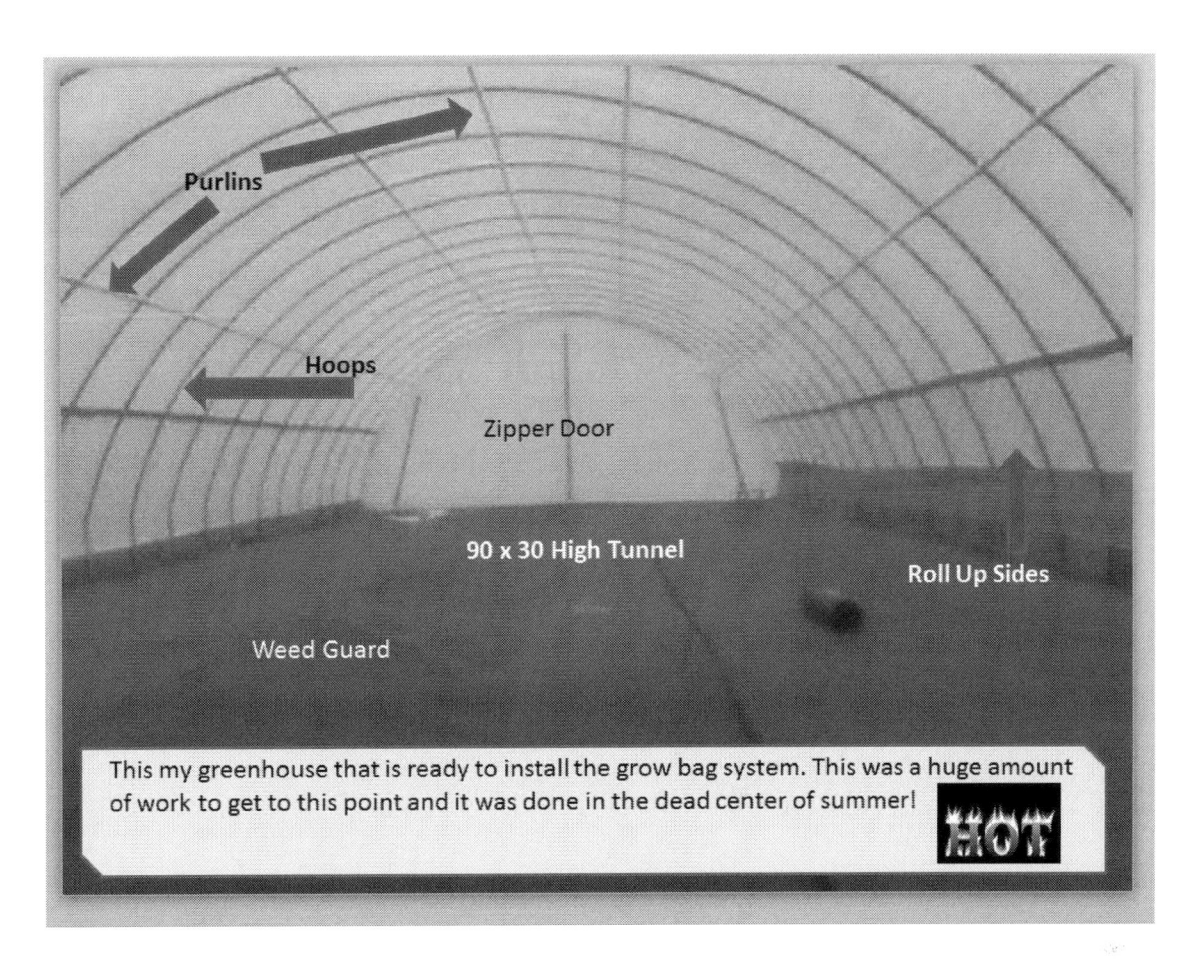

> Purlins
> Hoops
> Zipper Door
> 90 x 30 High Tunnel
> Roll Up Sides
> Weed Guard
>
> This my greenhouse that is ready to install the grow bag system. This was a huge amount of work to get to this point and it was done in the dead center of summer! HOT

Equipment

Besides the bags, I watered and fertilized the bags with a drip system which is diagramed below. I used one dripper at each bag. The drippers are a 1 gallon per hour type.

Cutoff valves ⊗
Grow Bags ▪

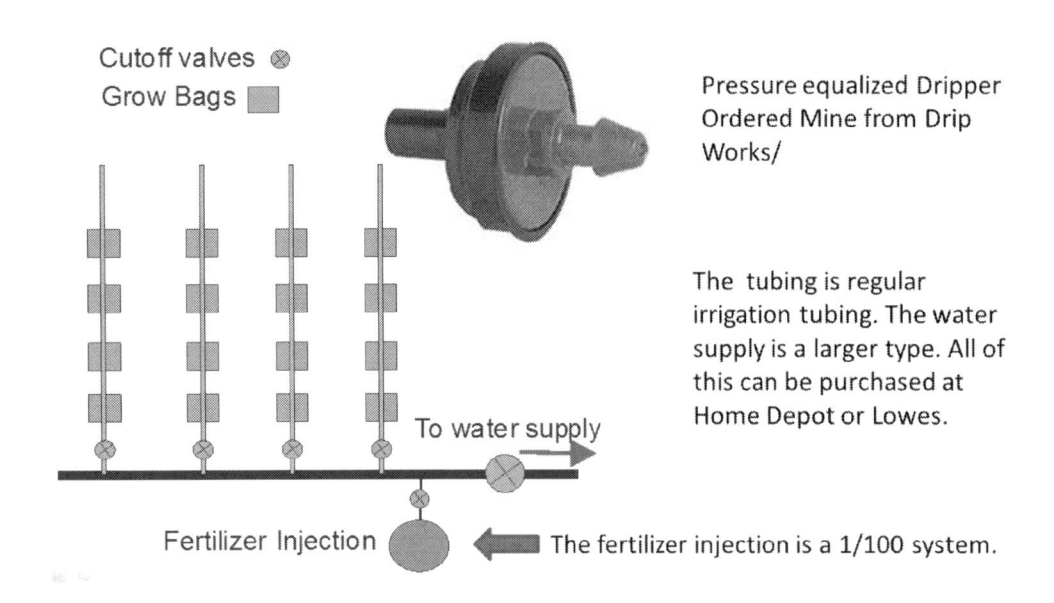

Pressure equalized Dripper Ordered Mine from Drip Works/

The tubing is regular irrigation tubing. The water supply is a larger type. All of this can be purchased at Home Depot or Lowes.

To water supply

Fertilizer Injection ⬅ The fertilizer injection is a 1/100 system.

Cheap fertilizer injection

　Besides the bags, I watered and fertilized the bags with a drip system which is diagramed below. I used one dripper at each bag. The drippers are a 1 gallon per hour type.

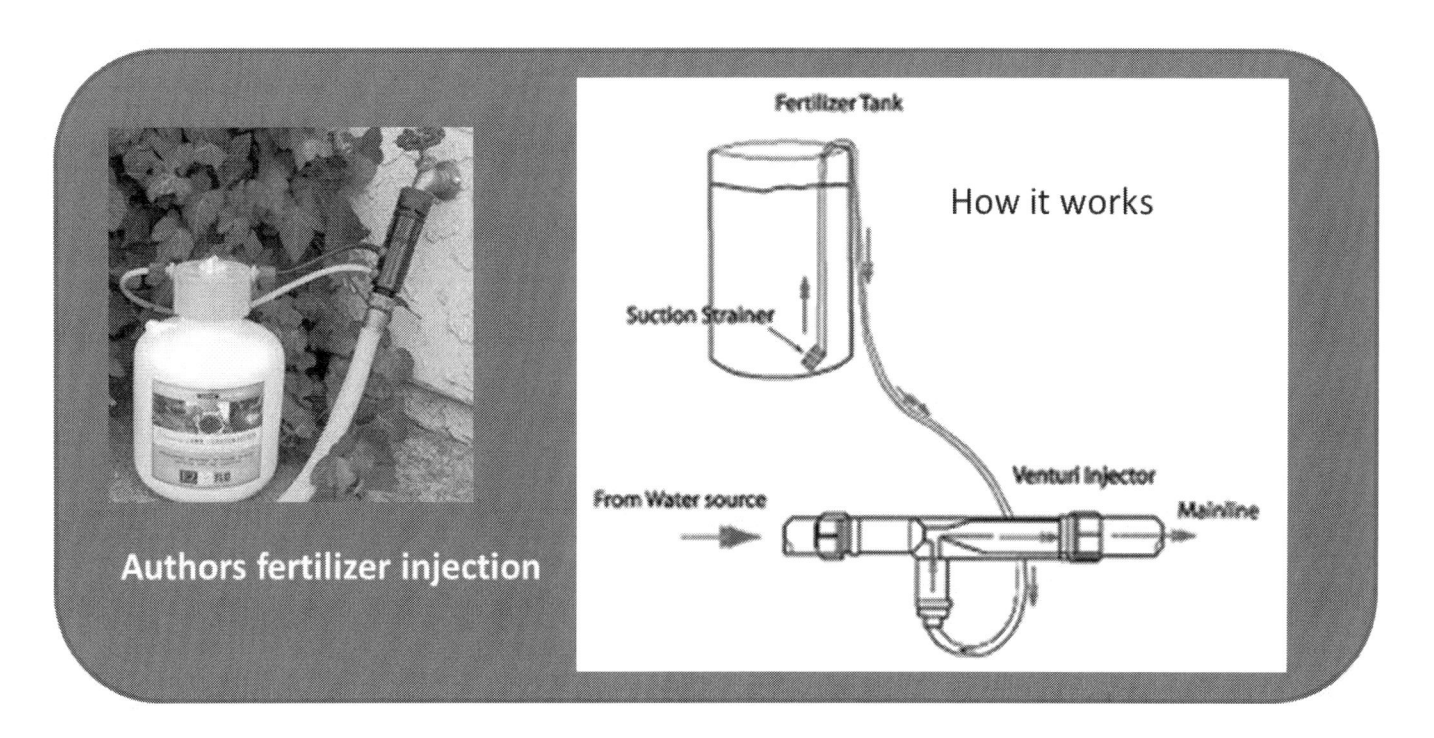

Authors fertilizer injection

How it works

The fertilizer injection is a 1/100 system. One part fertilizer to 100 parts water.

Growing Medium

Previously I used a mixture that seemed to have worked in 5 gallon grow bags 33% each of the following

- Pearlite
- Mushroom Compost
- Peat

If I were to do it again, I would use the following:

- Peat Mix – Pro Mix Brand – 50% of this with the compost
- Compost – your choice. I like horse manure compost.
- Worm Castings – 1 cup
- Additional Fertilizer – General purpose water solvable fertilizer + 1 table spoon of Magnesium Sulfate (Epsom Sault) added to the mixed fertilizer per gallon. Fertilize once a week and every 5 days during fruiting.

If you are in a grid down situation, you can always hand water and fertilize the grow bags

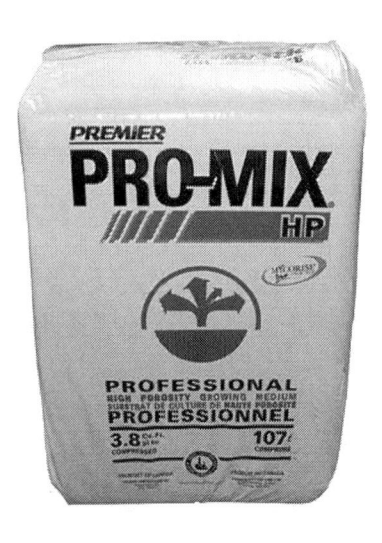

Tips Using Grow Bags

Why grow in grow bag?

The following are some good reasons:

- No weeding.
- You can put them in many different locations.
- Space Saving – you could put them on a stair case for vertical growing.
- Grow just about anything. Even carrots, potatoes (regular and sweet).
- Get growing quickly.

Suggested growing options. The use of cardboard minimizes weeds. The milk crates stabilize the grow bag. Hand water.

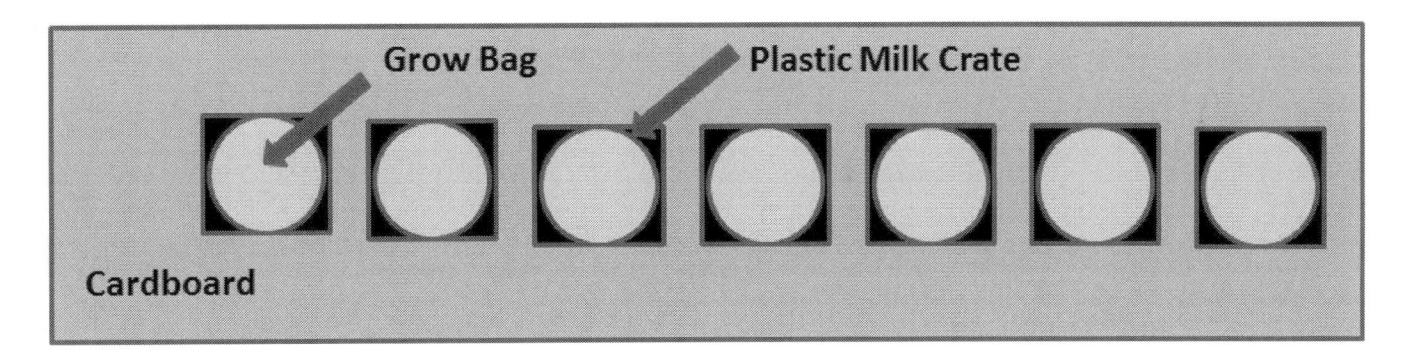

Not enough room – Here is a suggestion:

Grow Bag Stair Steps

I would suggest that you purchase a few hundred or more of the cheap grow bags and put them away in a cool dark place so they stay good as heat and UVB can destroy plastic quickly.

If you have the water and some compost, you will be able to grow much of your food with these bags.

Tip: put them on something you can move in case the weather gets really wild. Have some sort of structure that you can protect the grow bags if necessary like plastic of shade cloth.

Idea: The Grow Circle

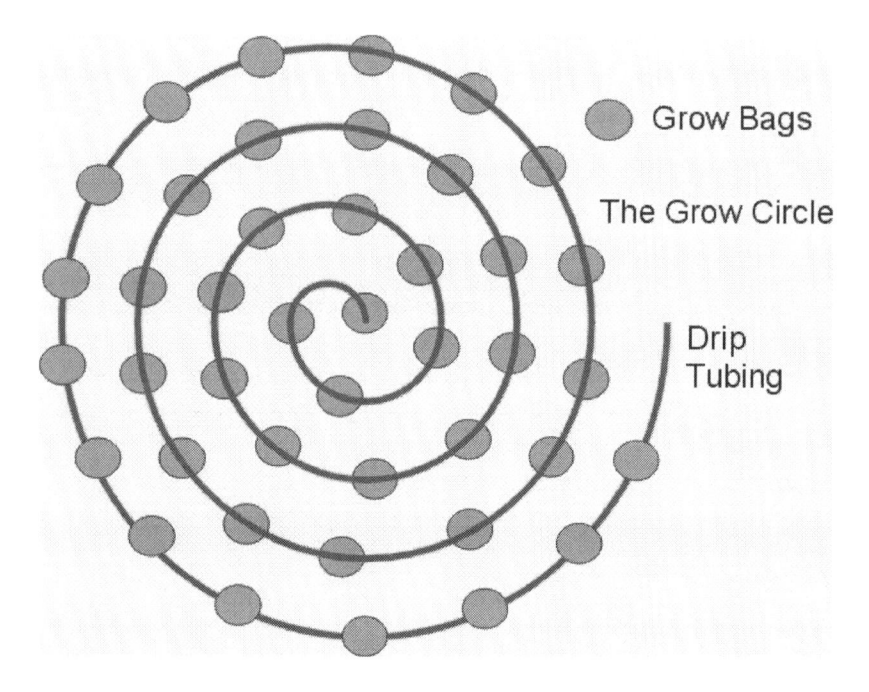

As you have seen what and where I used grow bags, they work wonderfully in a small or large greenhouse.

In a pinch, a grow bag can be lifted up on to something with wheels and moved or transported on some sort of vehicle. Start them in a greenhouse and taken outside or to another farm.

Kratky method

The answer to SGSM growing?

From Wikipedia, the free encyclopedia

The Kratky method is a passive hydroponic technique for growing plants suspended above a reservoir of nutrient-rich water. Because it is a non-circulating technique, no additional inputs of water or nutrients are needed after the original application, and no electricity, pumps, or water and oxygen circulation systems are required. The Kratky method has applications both for commercial food production and as a small-scale and low-maintenance technique for home growers

Plants are placed in net cups filled with an inert growth medium such as rock wool, hydroton, or coconut coir. The net cups are suspended above a reservoir of water containing essential nutrients in solution. Only the root tips are allowed to touch the surface of the reservoir. As the plant grows and depletes the water level, a gap of moist air will form and expand between the water surface and the base of the plant. The roots in this gap become laterally branching "oxygen roots," and absorb oxygen from the air inside the container. By the time the water level is fully depleted, the plant should be ready to harvest. Thus, in one growing cycle, no additional replenishment of water or nutrients is needed beyond the initial application.

The method is named after Bernard Kratky, a researcher at the University of Hawaii who first proposed the method in the journal Actae Horticulturae in 2009. In the article, Kratky discusses using floating pallets for commercial food production. Multiple plants are placed in net pots on boards that float atop a shared reservoir, with support beams slightly underneath the water level. As water is depleted, the boards eventually come to rest on the support beams, providing an air gap to allow oxygen intake. The Kratky method has also found popularity among home growers, and is often carried out on smaller scales in containers such as buckets and mason jars. The technique is designed for leafy vegetables that do not consume large amounts of water, so the water supply does not need to be continually replenished.

Below is my take on the Kratky Method or system, Kratky made this method popular,

but it has been around for thousands of years.

What if you lived in a place that was very arid and the soil was almost worthless for growing food? What if there was no electricity? What if you were very poor and had no means of feeding your family? But what if you had access to one of the following mediums?

- Coconut Fiber
- Gravel
- Rice hulls
- Sand
- Sawdust
- Volcanic Rock

With access to the above, a little water, clear and black plastic, some discarded truck tires or plastic drink or milk bottles, a few seeds and a little hydroponic fertilizer a person could provide food for their family. If they expanded their operation they could put some money in their pocket. While this does not sound like down town Dallas Texas, many millions of people all over the earth are faced with problems of good food, water and employment. Hydroponics may well be the answer to these problems if enough people care enough to spread the word. It is with that intention that this module on low energy systems is offered.

Note: Worm castings make good fertilizer mixed with compost. A compost tea could be made from this mixture and used as a nutrient.

Is it true?

Those of us who have been involved in hydroponics have always believed that it was necessary to circulate and aerate the nutrient applied to our plants. For the most part, this was done using air bubbling through the nutrient or by dropping the nutrient back into the nutrient tank from a small distance. Other systems spray a fine mist onto the roots which adds oxygen to the nutrient. Is this belief true? The answer to this question is yes. In most typical hydroponics systems this is necessary to prevent root rot and other problems. If one is to construct and use a no energy non-circulating hydroponics system them the system must be different and the approach must be new. There are a lot of advantages for taking this approach. First the systems are simple and are made from common and locally available materials. Second, they are low maintenance and if done properly can provide outstanding results. Third, they offer a very economical approach to growing food.

How does a non-circulating system work?

Farmers have been using this sort of technique perhaps for centuries, especially in Asia. It was noticed that plants that were planted in a built-up bed did quite well even in a very wet environment. Plants that were grown at ground level did just as well until heavy rains effectively drowned the plants. This is nothing new and any home grower knows that in a wet environment building up the beds provides for good drainage. But if one looks closer, the built up bed did very well even when the lower portion of the bed was very wet. One would expect that the roots would rot in this environment. Looking closer, it was also observed that the built-up part of the bed was made of very porous materials like dry grass and other materials that contained a large air space.

These two facts have led to a better understanding of a plant's root system. First, the built-up portion of the bed provided the plants' roots with a warm moist oxygen laden environment. The lower portion of the bed contains water and nutrient. Because there are two environments, the plant develops two types of root systems. The roots in the upper portion of the bed develop into "air roots" and provide the plant with most of its oxygen. The lower roots that either float or become immersed in the nutrient laden water become "wet roots". *Because the nutrient and water in this system has only a small amount of absorbed oxygen, the wet roots do not develop into the huge root mats we see in regular hydroponics systems.* The reason is that in a normal system oxygen, nutrients and water must come from the same set of roots.

In a non-circulating system, the air roots are larger than the wet roots. Because of this, the pH and EC of the nutrient are more stable. One other fact about plants' roots makes non-circulating hydroponics systems possible. First, roots can be ether air or wet roots. Mostly, roots start out as wet roots and once the wet environment is removed (moisture), the roots become air roots. This transformation into a air root from a wet root is a one way ride and immersing air roots in liquid will quickly kill the plant.

Characteristics of a Non-circulating Hydroponics system

First, the system must have two zones. The air zone that will hold the plant and will normally be composed of some inert medium. The medium holder could be a web pot, plastic cup, perforated PVC pipe or an aluminum soda can with the bottom removed. The medium could be a peat, perlite, vermiculite mixture. In areas where this is not available, simple grass clippings or rice hulls could be used.

The wet zone is composed of an air gap and the nutrient solution. The air gap provides some oxygen to the water and provides a warm, moist interface between the air roots and the nutrient.

Operation of a Non-circulating Hydroponics System

In this sort of system, the plants all start out taking up nutrient, water and oxygen. This is done by setting the wet zone high enough so that it comes in contact with the media and supplies the young plant nutrient by capillary action. As the plant grows, it will use nutrient and water and the wet zone will fall in the system. As the level falls, the exposed roots will convert into air roots. At some point, the level will drop below the medium, and the plant will grow wet roots that will float or be immersed in the water. If the system is growing a quick maturing plant like lettuce and there is enough nutrient and water in the system to last until harvest, then the level can be allowed to drop and no replacement of water or nutrients would be necessary. When plants that require a long growth period are used (like tomatoes), then the wet zone level must be monitored. In this case, keeping the wet zone 1 or 2 inches below the medium would be necessary. Because you will kill the plant if air roots are covered with water, some sort of float valve system should be used to keep the wet zone level at the proper place. Although non-circulating systems do not have the same level of pH and EC problems automated systems do, the pH and EC should be monitored if at all possible.

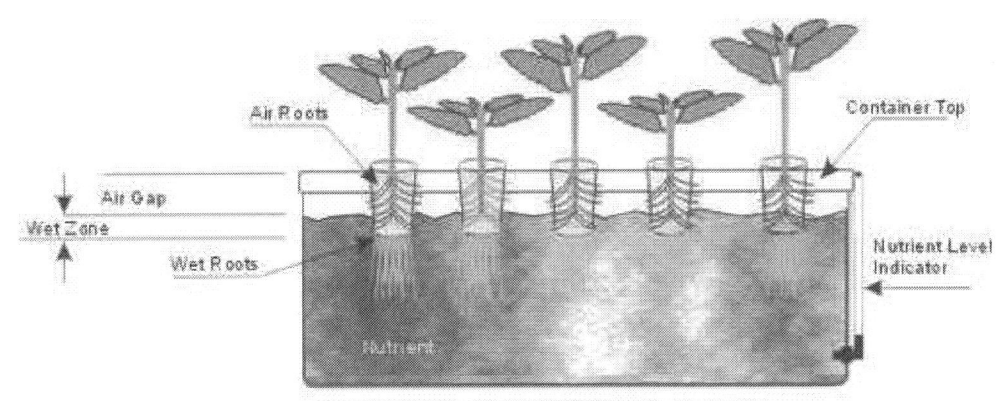

Wet Root Garden

You can build this system by using many of the plastic containers sold at department stores which are very inexpensive. You could also use a five gallon bucket and fewer plants. Cut holes in the top of the container or bucket that fit the medium holder and plant. This could be net pots or just simple plastic cups with holes punched in them. When first starting the system, make sure that the wet zone covers the bottom 1/3 of the medium holder. As the plant grows, let the water level fall until it is about 1 inch below the cups, and then keep it there by adding water. If you are growing quick harvest plants like lettuce, you may not need to add any liquid at all. Longer growing plants may need water. Monitor the pH and EC if possible.

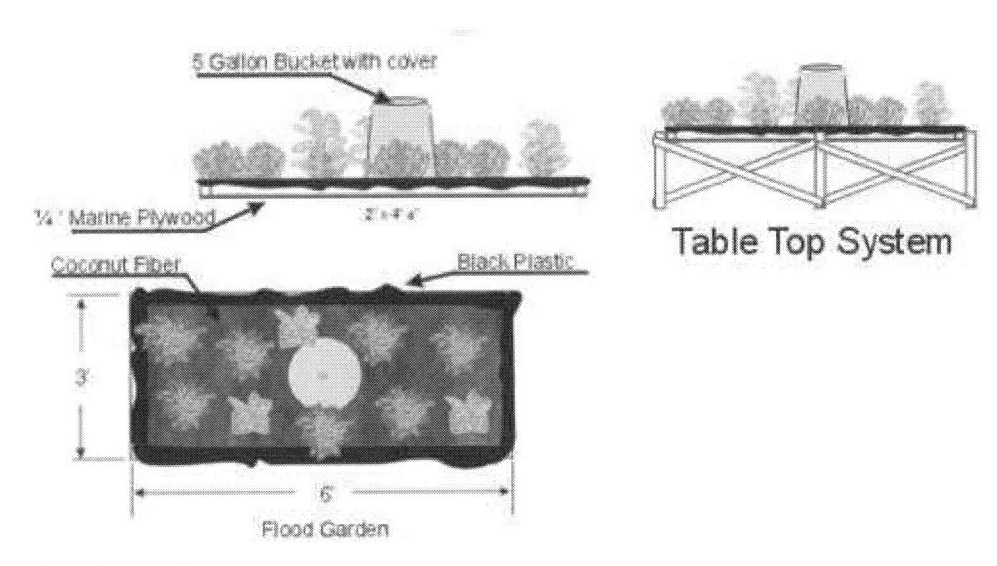

Flood Garden

The flood garden uses the same principles as the Simple Simon in the plans system. In this system, nutrient is fed to the system via a 5 gallon bucket that has a lid with a 3/4 inch hole in it. The system is composed of a box made up of 2 x 4's with a plywood bottom. two layers of 6 mil black plastic is laid out in the box and stapled to the sides. An inert medium like coconut fiber or other available medium can be used to cover the container. A small stick is placed under one side of the 5 gallon bucket to allow it to fill the container with a small layer of nutrient. As the plants take up water, the nutrient level will drop and more water will be released by the bucket. This system can be built on the ground or on a table top.

Make sure the system is level. The hole in the bucket should be an inch or so from the side of the bucket.

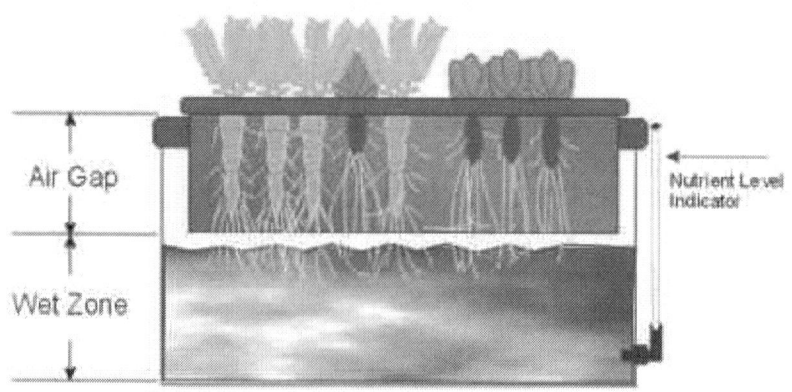

Root Box
   The root box is a design that allows for growing of root vegetables like carrots or other plants. This system is essentially a box within a box. The inner box contains the medium and although not shown, the bottom is perforated with holes every 1/4". These holes allow the roots to grow out of the container and into the wet zone. The bottom of the container also makes a root barrier, the plant thinks it is in soil and grows along the perforated bottom creating a large air zone root system. The outer plastic container holds the nutrient and the level indicator. A hole is cut out of this containers' lid which takes the inner container. Make sure all the containers are thick enough to stop transmission of light. You might want to use black plastic inside the nutrient container for this purpose. To operate this system, fill the inner container with medium. This could be a mixture of perlite and coconut fiber or other mixtures. Fill the nutrient tank until the level is an inch or so into the medium. Through

capillary action, the medium will be moist, and contribute water and nutrient to the new plant. As the plants grow, the nutrient level will fall.

Once it is about 1 inch below the medium, it is imperative that you keep it at this level. Never over water, as this may kill the plants.

Note: a lot of short length carrots are now available and would work well in such a system.

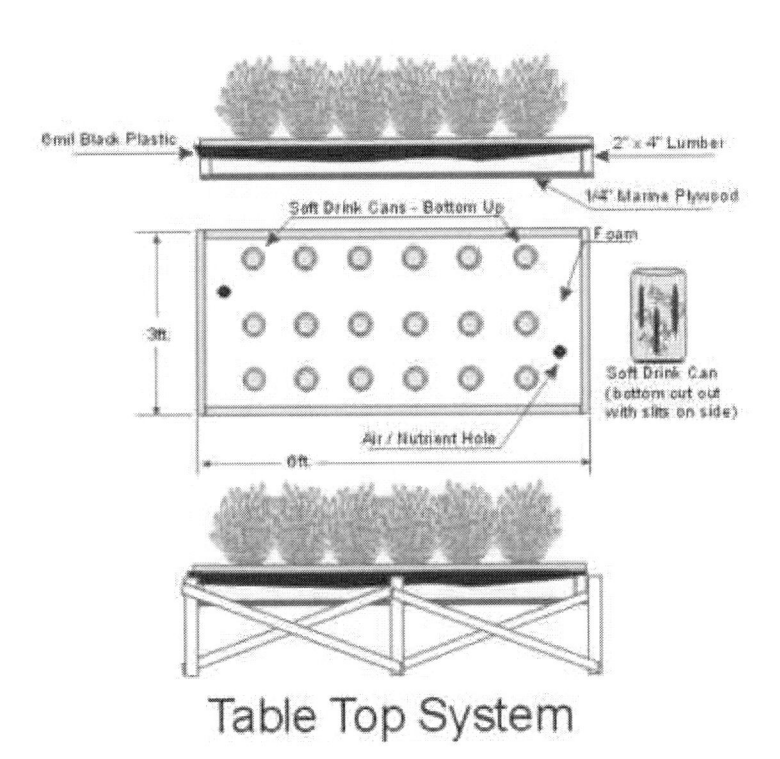

Table Top System

Soft Drink Garden
   The Soft Drink Garden is made from a 2 x 4 frame, with a plywood bottom and lined with 2 layers of 6 mil black plastic. For large plants (tomatoes etc.) use 2 x 6 lumber. After making the frame, lay in the plastic and staple it to the sides. Then cut a piece of foam insulation obtained at your local home center to fit the top of the frame. Depending on the final size of the plants you will grow, cut out holes to take aluminum soft drink cans. Fill the container to a three inch level with nutrient. Cut the bottom of soft drink cans with a hand held can opener. Cut 2 or 3 long slits down the sides of the can. Fill the cans with media and a seed or a plant transplant and then insert into the holes of the foam. Monitor the nutrient level, and try to keep it at a 2 inch level.

To check root growth you can lift up one side of the foam. Check your nutrient level with a dry stick. Add water and nutrient as necessary.

Low – No Cost Systems

I know I must get on that "last nerve" as my wife repeats when I stop in a store or take out the trash. It seems that I see hydroponics systems everyplace I look. If you think about it, just what is a no energy hydroponics system? It usually consists of a container that holds a medium that a plant can grow in when you add a nutrient. You can let the plant decide how much nutrient it needs by some sort of wick or air / nutrient system. If you want a drip system, then you can give your valuable plants a drink every day and collect the nutrient from the bottom of that 2-liter bottle you are using to hold the medium. You may ask how is this any different from growing in dirt? The real difference is the environment. It is much more controlled and protected. If it is dry, you don't need rain. If there is a storm it isn't washed away. And the best part of all is that they are simple. No energy hydroponics systems are so simple that even the smallest child could operate one. Could you imagine how much produce could be grown if everyone in your neighborhood had one simple system? Our whole JIT (just in time) system of food delivery is flawed. Yes it works, but what if the truck cannot move that lettuce or spinach or those red tomatoes across the country to your local store? In the future (because of energy costs and other environmental problems), simple and small hydroponics systems could produce a large amount of our food. And local (close to the city) commercial hydroponics businesses could provide locally what we now move using expensive energy over thousands of miles.

"No-energy hydroponics system is so simple that even the smallest child could operate one". The milk container system above is an example of such a system. The milk container and plastic pot were free and had been tossed out. The media and nutrient cost very little. This system will produce lettuce and herbs for many months if cared for. Think what 50 or 80 of these could do!

The "No-energy hydroponics systems (see above) are also simple. The strawberries and herbs are both hand watered with nutrient when needed. Both of them use a perlite / coconut fiber mixture. The strawberry bag has holes at the bottom to allow excess nutrient to drip out. This nutrient is collected and used again. Most small root plants can be grown in a tray. Scallions, radishes, lettuce and chives come to mind. Even small patio tomatoes would work.

Hydroponics – The Answer to Hunger
The following graphics and some text were taken from the PowerPoint presentation Women of Hope Project

Types of substrates.

- Rice hulls
- Sand
- Gravel
- Sawdust
- Coco Coir Fiber
- Almond, pistachio and peanut shells
- Red Volcanic Rock

On a rooftop:

Old Tires:

Discarded plastic containers:

Gardens and Gardening

Raised Beds

Raised Beds

If you're using wood make sure it's not treated with chemicals!

Above photo from Brooke Edmunds. Copyright CC BY-SA 2.0

So what are some of the advantages of Raised Bed gardening?

There are many good things about a raised or elevated garden. **If they are made tall enough you won't have to bend over much to maintain, start or harvest.** What I like about them is the following

- Fewer weeds and easier to dispatch!
- It's your newly created soil and you can add the best organic compost you can get your hands on.
- Easily hand watered if kept small.
- Soil Drains better than flat soil based gardens
- If kept small they can be placed near to your home or all over the place.

I could go on and there are many virtues of a raised or elevated bed.

How to make them.

If you have wood, a saw a hammer and some nails you are on your way.

Another example below:

Author of above picture is Kerstin Namuth. Copyright Creative Commons Attribution-Share Alike 4.0 International license.

Straw Bed Gardening – Hay Bed Gardening

Hey Hey Hay!

Photo by Colling-architektur. Copyright Creative Commons Attribution-Share Alike 3.0 Unported license.

How to get started with Straw Bed Gardening

Turn your new bail on its side. Make sure that your bale is week killer free as this will just kill most anything you plant in the bail. Do not remove the string or metal holding the bail together.

Water the bale. Watering will cause the bail to start to decompose and inside the bail will heat up. Inside the bail will get so hot that it would kill a plant. The answer is to condition the bale before you plant. This process usually takes around two or at most three weeks. For the first 3 or 4 days just water the bale completely (just make sure it stays wet). After about four days, water and add a liquid fertilizer to the bail. Most fertilizers that can be mixed with water can be added to a gallon of water. Read your instructions for the amounts. Simply add a capful or so to a gallon of water and pour it all on the bale. Do this for about a week.

Planting the bale

Make sure after two or three weeks the inside of the bail has cooled sown (less than 100F). Remove straw to form a hole that is as deep as the roots of your plant. If you are planting tomato plants, then just plant them just like you would do in soil. You can use good compost along with the plants if you wish. Make sure straw or soil covers the plants root system. Then water the plant (plants) well.

Water and fertilize the bail on a regular basis

Because the bale has few nutrients, it's important to fertilize them every week or two. You'll also want to make sure not to let the bale dry out. Note if you over fertilize you will get great green leafs but nothing else.

Happy Bail Growing – Note you can grow most anything in a bale. Good news, use the bail to make compost after using or reusing.

Ruth Stout Garden

Nicknamed the "Mulch Queen", Ruth Stout was born in the United States in 1884. As early as 1920, she realized that all traditional methods of working with the soil (digging, weeding, watering, plowing, hoeing), could be replaced by simply adding a layer of hay on the ground.

Ruth Stout's no-work gardening method recommends using heavy mulch to maintain a weedless garden.

Photo by Gardenworks

The Ruth Stout garden is my favorite.

God Bless Ruth Stout

This garden can be built in one season and you can start growing in 6 months. It's called the Ruth Stout method. It's a no dig, minimum maintenance garden. I don't plan to look pretty during the SGSM and my garden won't either. It will just work.

My Ruth Stout garden started with any type of green matter or animal manure (no human, cat or dog) I could get my hands on. I even went to Home Depot and purchased sacks of processed cow manure. We have two horses which also supplied great quantities of manure. The trees dumped copious amounts of leafs. I collected them all. The dirt here is really rocky, but this method really doesn't care because I will never use a shovel on the soil. You could do this on the worst soil around and still be successful.

I was in luck, just as I started looking for more compost, my neighbor across the street contacted me and said he could provide a huge amount of horse manure and hay two times a week. They probably have over 40 horses!

The first step is to arrange all this collected matter onto cardboard beds (kills weeds). **I dumpster dive for my cardboard.** After you have built up the bed with 4 or five inches of your collection of green matter, manures and anything organic, put a layer of hay about a foot and a half deep over the beds. – Then you wait. If in the fall, let the beds cook. Add water if it's very dry. In the spring (about 6 months later) you can plant. To grow potatoes (get the short season ones) just roll back the hay and toss your potato starts on your new soil and then recover with the hay. Water if necessary. This method saves water and you may not have to water at all if you received rain while it was cooking. I just did a large garden doing this, and even after 3 months, the soil being created under the hay look amazing.

Note I grab all the free coffee grounds I can for my mulch.

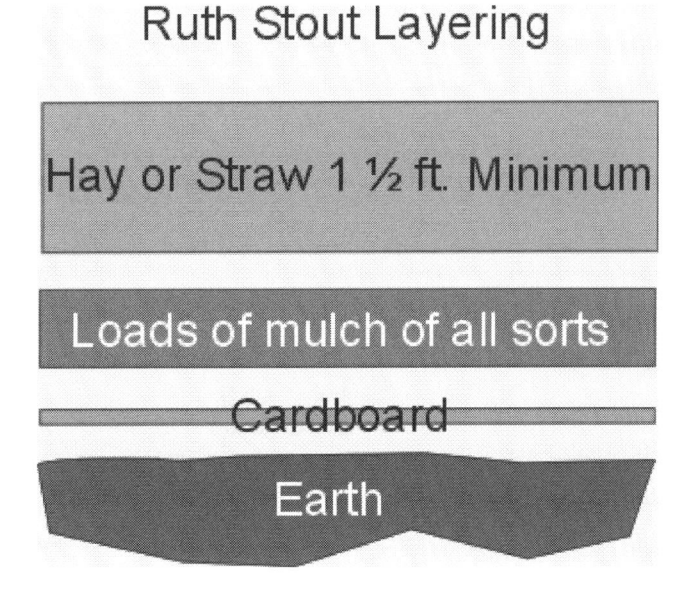

Ruth Stout Layering

- Hay or Straw 1 ½ ft. Minimum
- Loads of mulch of all sorts
- Cardboard
- Earth

Planting in a Ruth Stout garden is easy as pulling back the hay and inserting your starts into the new soil after which you need to pull the hay around the start. For seeds, part the hay and plant. Wait for germination and growth and then pull the hay around your new plants. If you wish, you can add compost to your plants, but always under the hay. After a while you will have to add new hay as it decays and becomes your new soil. This method works even if you don't add compost. At harvest time always return the plant back on to the soil. That way you will be adding organic matter all the time. It's not pretty but it works.

Advantages of a SGSM Ruth Stout garden:

- No digging.
- Creates new soil.
- Can be put into production quickly.
- Way less work and minimal weeding.
- Less or no watering may be needed.
- Protects the plant roots from heat and cold.
- Works well on useless or very poor soil.
- Frees up time to do other survival things.
- Works well when growing winter crops which can hide in the hay.

So what can you grow in a Ruth Stout garden? In normal times and in normal weather you can grow just about anything. Things like corn to tomatoes and everything in between. But the question we should be asking is what types and cultivars should we have seed for during the SGSM? I will have a seed list at the end of this section. Growing from seed in the soil will be tough as it will be a slow start. Try to only grow from starts as these give weeks of gained time and speeds up growth in the garden. So here are some examples: Make the beds wide enough so you can work each side easily. (4 ft.)

- Plants that have a short growing season – perhaps 50 days or less.
- Cold tolerant plants,
- Plants that grow in low light levels.
- Plants that you have starts for that were grown in a small greenhouse or protected environment. Get them as large as practical.
- Grow a large numbers of plants that have high nutrient levels.
- Vegetables that can be stored (potatoes, carrots squash and other things).

Vegetables crops that will grow in light to partial shade are: arugula, beets, broccoli, Brussels sprouts, cabbage, carrots, cauliflower, celery, chard, Chinese cabbage, corn salad, endive, escarole, garlic, horseradish, kale, kohlrabi, leaf lettuce, leeks, mustard, New Zealand spinach, parsnips, peas, potatoes, radishes, rutabagas, scallions, sorrel, spinach, turnips, and watercress.

Vegetables that will tolerate light to partial shade include: bush beans, summer squash, and determinate or bush tomatoes adapted to cool regions or ready for harvest in 55 days or so.

Herbs that will grow in light to partial shade are: basil, catnip, chervil, chives, cress, horseradish, lemon balm, mint, parsley and rosemary

The problem with any of the above is how many days to maturity? Many of the leafy vegetables can be eaten before maturity. Note, the problem should not be shade but very cloudy days with some or reduced light. Tomatoes could be a real problem so just choose the small ones as the large beefy ones may not make it (pick them green).

TIP

Green tomatoes really store well. One harvest season I probably had 50 lbs. of green tomatoes. I put them in a cardboard box in a cool place and covered them. I made sure that they did not touch each other. They all eventually matured, and we ate the green ones as well. It took over two months to eat them all. You might think about

* * * *

Growing food may become a crap shoot during the SGSM

* * * *

Homework

A homework assignment: Go through or order seed catalogs. With a felt tip pen mark seed that you may be interested in. Make sure its practical and pay close attention to the days to maturity and the possibility of storage. Look at what I have recommended (I am not a cold weather growing expert) and then order your seeds. Think 7 years of seed. Seeds store well when they are very cool or even frozen. Order a paperback book on seed saving. It's very easy to do and practical. You don't have much time left to prepare. While you are working at your day-to-day job, never forget what is coming and how far behind you are. Do something every day to prepare. Look at those around you. Do they know what you know? Probably not and would they even believe you? Stay focused and make a check list. If you live in New York or the East Coast I would think about moving. You will know soon enough. Even the blind and deaf will understand by 2020-2021. You will have that many years to get ahead by starting now while things are relatively inexpensive (and quiet).

Here are my suggestions on seed. They are based on 70 days (a bit over two months) of warm growing weather. Use your greenhouse to extend your growing season and grow your starts. Using starts can get you growing two weeks into the growing season or more. There are more vegetables that you could grow so you might want to add to this list. I don't have corn on the list. While fresh corn is good, it takes a lot longer to dry it. Also wind can damage corn. I will let you choose the cultivars. Just do your homework.

- Bush Beans – All are mostly 60 days
- Pole beans – 63 to 65 days
- Beets – 35 to 65 days
- Cabbage – 65 to 100 days. May not get full heads but cold hardy
- Carrots – 60 to 100 days, but carrots do well in colder weather if protected. Can even be dug out while covered in snow.
- Collards – 50 to 70 days but are cold hardy. Highly recommended
- Celery – probably not, but cutting (Chinese) celery would be OK
- Cucumbers – 50 to 75 days. Poor nutrient value but good tasting!
- Egg Plant – 60 to 65 days
- Kale – 50 to 60 days – Cold weather hardy. Highly recommended
- Leek – Grow in the greenhouse
- Lettuce – 50 to 65 days. You can pick lleaf lettuce as it grows over time.
- Melons – 70 to 100 days. Iffy?
- Mustard – 45 to 60 days. Can be eaten at any stage. Always grow mustard.
- Peppers – all types 65 to 100 days. Very good for you and can be dried
- Pumpkins – 65 to 120 days. Iffy?
- Radish – 25 to 65 days. This should always be grown. Can eat as a microgreen or a full grown plant. Really healthy eating.
- Spinach – 25 to 45 days. Always grow this.
- Summer squash – 50 to 65 days. Always grow this. I like the large round 8 Ball zucchini
- Turnip and turnip greens – 55 days. Good for you
- Winter Squash – 60 to 110 days – Always grow the long storage types like Waltham Squash.
- Tomatoes – 65 to 120 days. Require a lot of heat and sun shine. Grow smaller type tomatoes. Think about growing larger tomatoes and harvest green. They store will (up to two months) in the house.
- Herbs – Grow a large variety in pots. Bring in if it gets too cool or cold.

Square Foot Gardening
From Wikipedia, the free encyclopedia

Square foot gardening is the practice of dividing the growing area into small square sections (typically 1 foot on a side, hence the name). The aim is to assist the planning and creating of a small but intensively planted vegetable garden. It results in a simple and orderly gardening system, from which it draws much of its appeal. Mel Bartholomew coined the term "square foot gardening" in his 1981 book of the same name.

Each square is planted with a different crop species based on a formulation of either one, four, nine or sixteen plants per square depending on the plant's overall size. Once a "square foot" is harvested, a different crop can be planted for a continual harvest. To encourage a variety of different crops in succession, and to discourage pests, each square is used for a different kind of plant (crop rotation) within the growing season. The number of plants per square depends on an individual plant's size. For example, a single tomato plant takes a full square, as might herbs such as oregano, basil or mint, while lettuce plants would be planted four per square, and up to sixteen per square of plants such as radish or carrots. Tall plants are trellised on the north side of the bed to avoid shading smaller plants and prevent sprawling on the ground.

One advantage of densely planted crops is that they can form a living mulch and can also prevent weeds from establishing or even germinating. Also, natural insect repellent methods such as companion planting (e.g. planting marigolds or other naturally pest-repelling plants) become more efficient in a close space, which may reduce the need to use pesticides. The large variety of crops in a small space also prevents plant diseases from spreading easily [1]

Since the beds are typically small, making covers or cages to protect plants from pests, cold, wind or too much sun is more practical than with larger gardens. To extend the growing season of a square foot garden, a cold/hot frame may be built around it, and by facing the cold/hot frame south, the SFG captures more light and heat during the colder months of spring and winter.

Below is an example of a squared off raised bed. Note the PVC hoops that will provide some protection if needed. Plastic Greenhouse plastic, frost shield and even shade cloth could be used.

Graphic above copyright Creative Commons Attribution-Share Alike 4.0 International license.

Is this a method for growing during the SGSM, you bet it is, especially if built as shown above with the built in protection.

Soils? Well you can use any organic soil that you may purchase or even better yet produce on your property.

What I like about this type of gardening is the intensity and ease of management. It's much easier to focus on a small plot of soil and plants than a huge expansive one.

Hugelkultur raised bed

Sketch of the layers of materiel involved in a Hugelkultur raised bed is shown below. **Graphic from Wikipedia and marked as GNU Free**. Hugelkultur is a horticultural technique where a mound constructed from decaying wood debris and other compostable biomass plant materials is later (or immediately) planted as a raised bed. Adopted by permaculture advocates, it is suggested the technique helps to improve soil fertility, water retention, and soil warming, thus benefiting plants grown on or near such mounds. Note: This method does not necessarily have to be a raised rounded bed bed, and most people who use this method only put a small layer flatly on top of the bed.

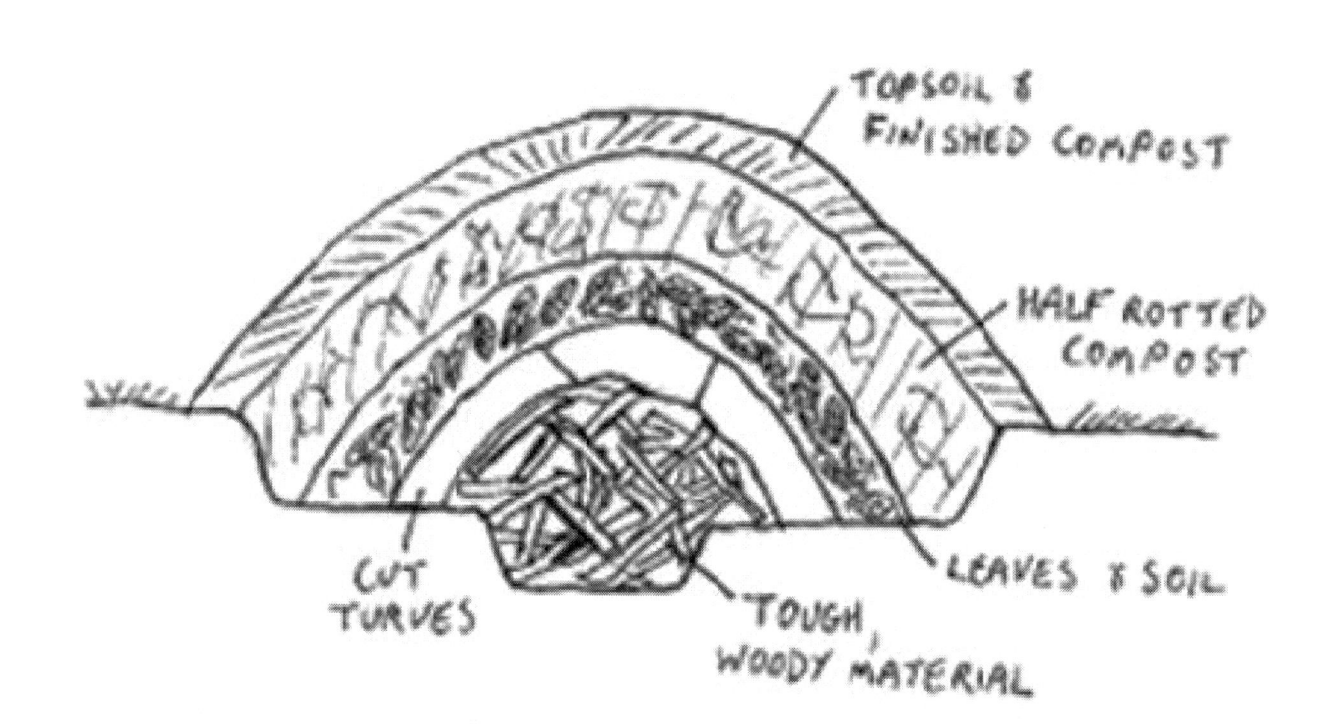

Hügelkultur bed prior to being covered with soil

Graphic by: Jon Roberts from Austin TX, USA. Licensed under the Creative Commons Attribution-Share Alike 2.0 Generic license.

Planting

The mound is left to rest for several months before planting, although some advise immediate planting.

Anything can be grown on the raised beds, but if the bed will decompose/release its nutrients quickly (so long as it is not made of bulky materials like tree trunks), more demanding crops such as pumpkins, cucumbers, cabbages, tomatoes, sweet corn, celery, or potatoes are grown in the first year, after which the bed is used for less demanding crops like beans, peas, and strawberries.

Lifespan

The original German publications described the mounds as having a lifespan of 5–6 years, after which they had to be rebuilt from scratch.

Microgreen Growing

Growing microgreens for your family.

Microgreens

How to grow, harvest and use them

Microgreens grow Quickly

Microgreens
- Broccoli 12 days
- Most Radish 7 to 10 days
- Arugula 14 days
- Cilantro 16 to 20 days (2nd. Leaf)
- Beet 16 days
- Carrot 16 to 20 days
- Kale 10 to 15 days

Microgreens
- Mustards 10 to 15 days
- Chard 10 to 15 days
- Cabbage 10 to 15 days
- Collards 10 to 15 days

Sprouts, Tendrils and Shoots
- Alfalfa 3 to 5 days
- Mung Bean 4 to 5 days
- Pea Tendril 7 to 14 days
- Sunflower Shoots 7 to 14 days

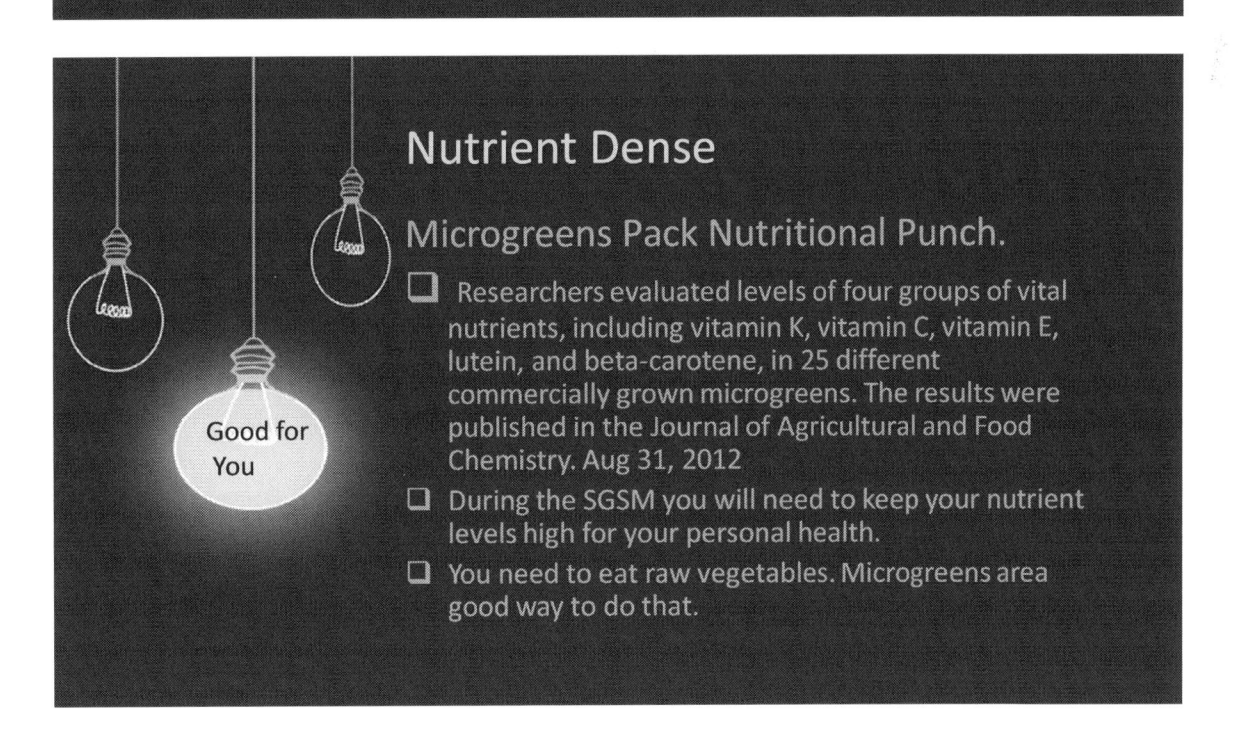

Nutrient Dense

Microgreens Pack Nutritional Punch.
- ☐ Researchers evaluated levels of four groups of vital nutrients, including vitamin K, vitamin C, vitamin E, lutein, and beta-carotene, in 25 different commercially grown microgreens. The results were published in the Journal of Agricultural and Food Chemistry. Aug 31, 2012
- ☐ During the SGSM you will need to keep your nutrient levels high for your personal health.
- ☐ You need to eat raw vegetables. Microgreens area good way to do that.

Food

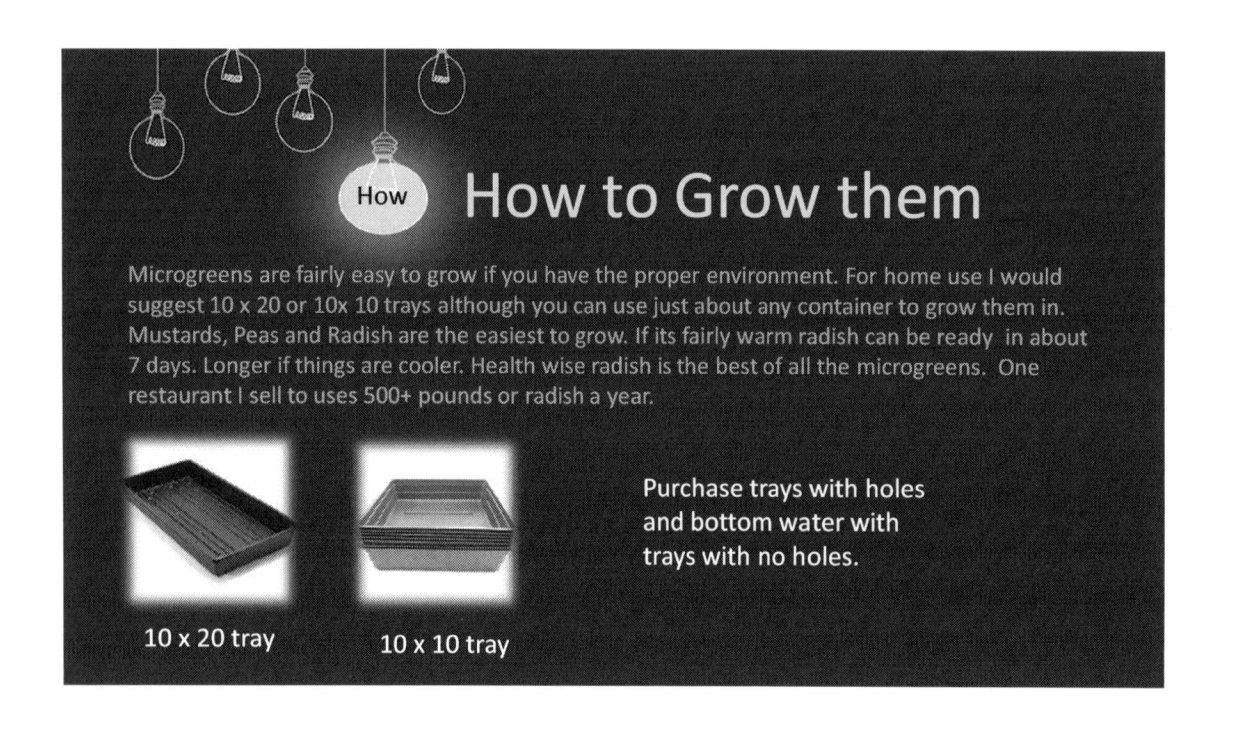

Microgreens go with anything or just by them selves.

Suggestion:
- Keep small trays of Pea Shoots and Sunflower shoots in your kitchen.
- Keep a continuous supply growing.
- Eat them raw.
- Mostly microgreens are eaten raw.

Carrot Microgreens

How to Grow them

Microgreens are fairly easy to grow if you have the proper environment. For home use I would suggest 10 x 20 or 10x 10 trays although you can use just about any container to grow them in. Mustards, Peas and Radish are the easiest to grow. If its fairly warm radish can be ready in about 7 days. Longer if things are cooler. Health wise radish is the best of all the microgreens. One restaurant I sell to uses 500+ pounds or radish a year.

Purchase trays with holes and bottom water with trays with no holes.

10 x 20 tray   10 x 10 tray

Growing Medium

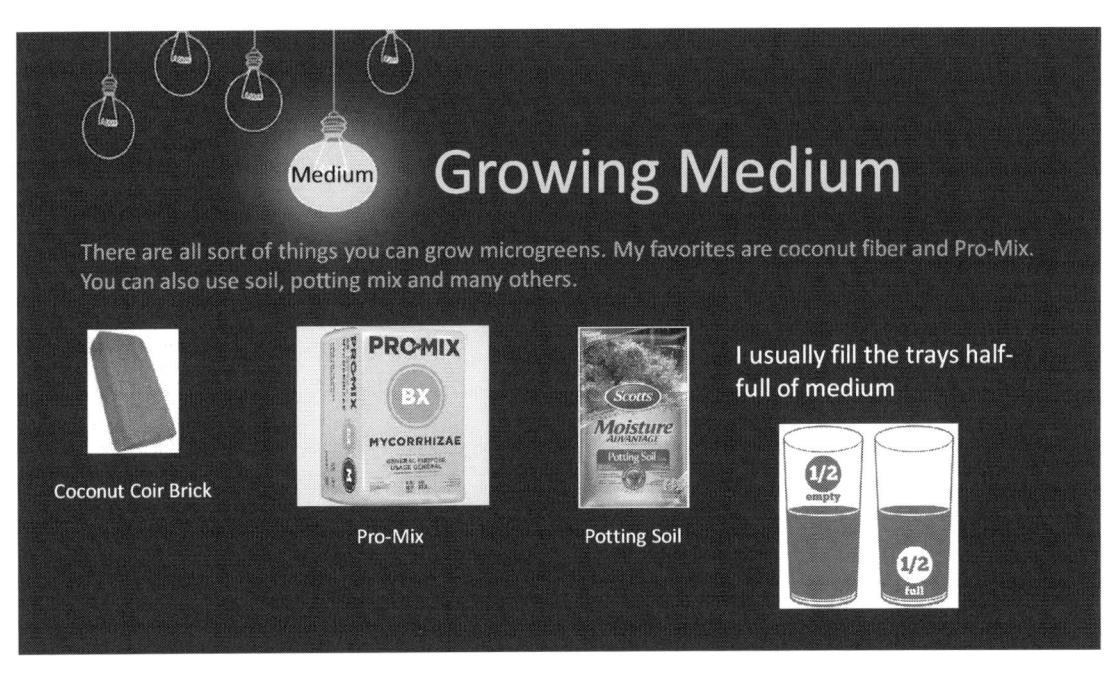

There are all sort of things you can grow microgreens. My favorites are coconut fiber and Pro-Mix. You can also use soil, potting mix and many others.

Coconut Coir Brick

Pro-Mix

Potting Soil

I usually fill the trays half-full of medium

Planting (Seeding)

Here are the steps:
- Half fill a 10 x 20 tray with no holes with water.
- Put about ¾ inch of coconut fiber evenly in each tray you want to seed (with holes)
- With the mister attachment, evenly water the coconut fiber. Just dampen it.
- Put the tray with coconut fiber in the tray with water. Let soak for a bit but not too long until the fiber is really wet but not soaked.
- Seed each tray with the density in the tray displayed on the right.
- Mist the evenly spaced seed with the mister. Water heavy but do not saturate.
- Seeded tray. I use between 7 and 8 table spoons of seed per tray.

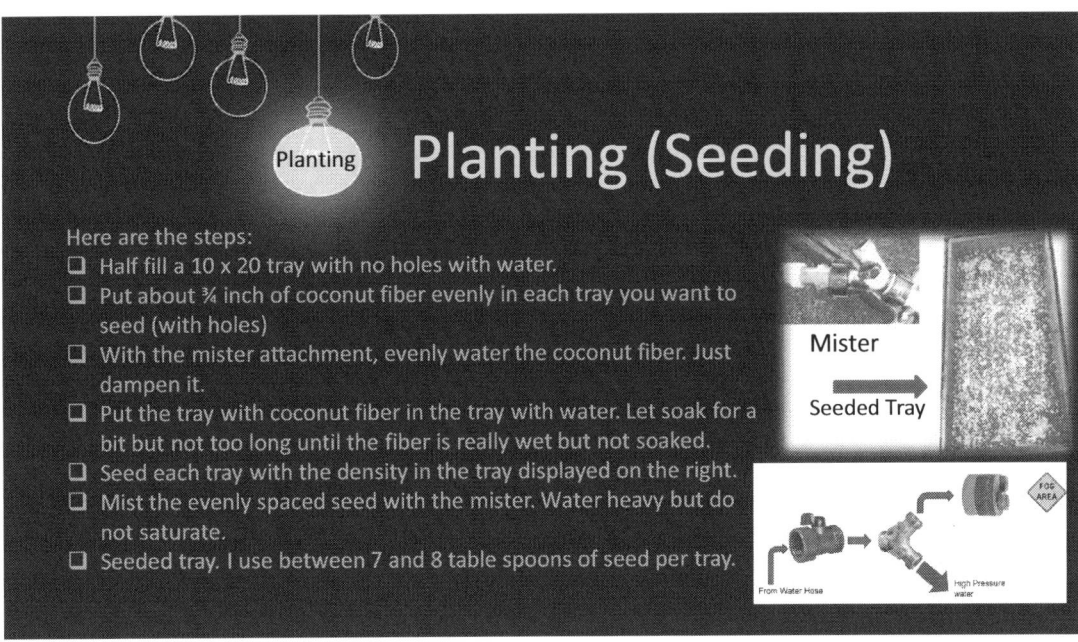

Growing

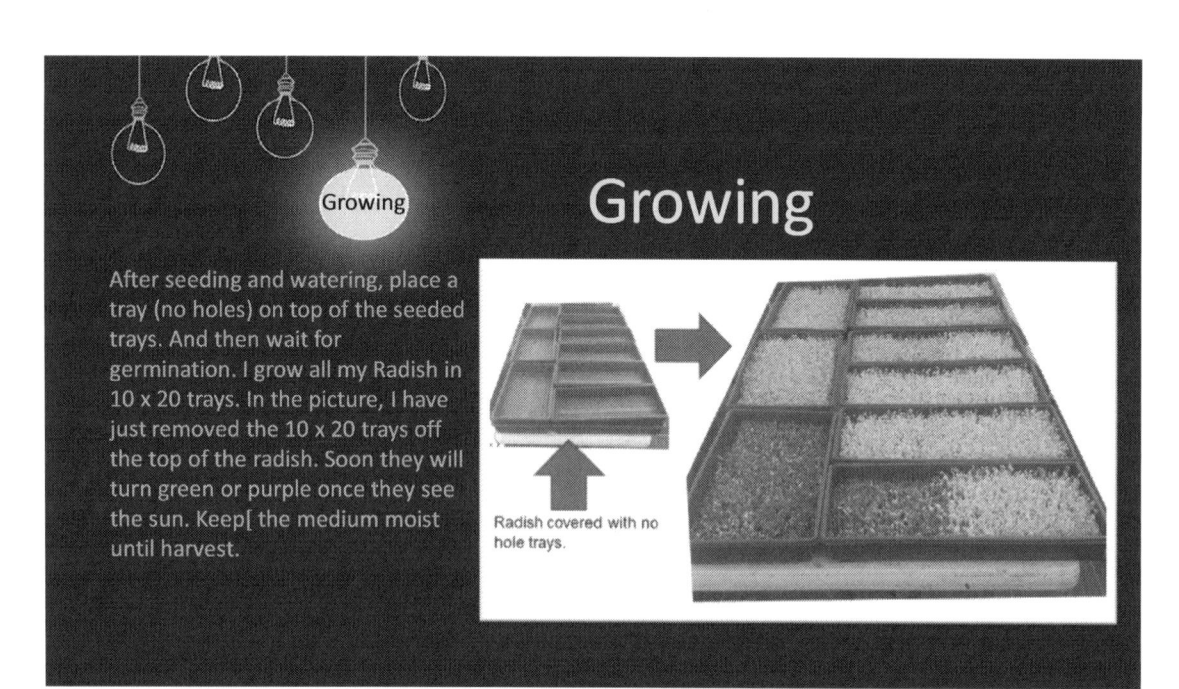

After seeding and watering, place a tray (no holes) on top of the seeded trays. And then wait for germination. I grow all my Radish in 10 x 20 trays. In the picture, I have just removed the 10 x 20 trays off the top of the radish. Soon they will turn green or purple once they see the sun. Keep[the medium moist until harvest.

Radish covered with no hole trays.

Harvesting

Once your microgreens have reached the size for harvesting, I use (clean) scissors to harvest. Microgreens grow fast and you might want to harvest the whole tray and place them in a refrigerator.

Harvesting

Medium Warning ⚠

Using composted things in growing can introduce an external possibility of harmful things that may get on or in your microgreens. I don't ever use composted animal manures. Its your choice though!

Always use new and clean media. The trays you use should be washed if reused and very clean. I use hydrogen Peroxide on my trays and bleach and soap to clean my trays. Always use gloves and clean your hands. Use a clean environment to grow and harvest. Make sure you scissors are thoroughly clean. Always use non-GMO seeds. Use the same seed provider who you know guarantees their seeds. Organic or non-organic seeds.

Last Things

- Nutrient Dense ☑
- Quickly Grown ☑
- Tasty ☑
- How ☑
- Minimum Energy input
- Minimum effort

Minimum Energy input
Microgreens don't take a huge amount of light to grow. There is a section on this in the course. A sunny window is usually good enough.

Minimum effort
Growing microgreens is a minimum effort way of growing. After seeding, the only thing that must be done is to keep the medium damp. And then comes harvest.

That's All

Gallery

| My favorite shirt | Fennel | Red Vein Sorrel |

Gallery

| Nasturtiums NASTYs but good | Red Vein Sorrel | Germinated Peas |

Gallery

| Red Amaranth | Author (Grumpy Grandpa) |

Here is my most favorite place to get microgreen seeds. I would suggest that you purchase in bulk as in pound sizes as Microgreens take a lot of seeds. One nifty thing about your microgreen seeds is that they can be used out in your regular garden.

Here is the URL for where I purchase seeds.

Trays

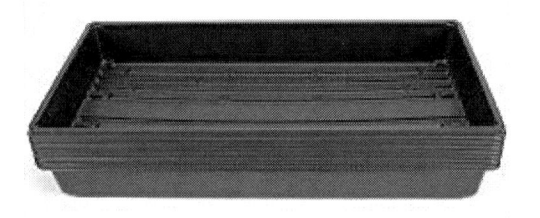

URL for no Holes Trays

URL for Trays with Holes

Vertical Gardening Ideas

Here are some ideas on vertical vegetable gardening. If you are an old pro, you have grown your climbing green beans on a trellis. This is a good example of vertical gardening.

The advantage of this method is of course that it saves space and is more easily managed by someone like me who is 76 years old!

Obviously a Vertical vegetable garden is an easy way to productively boost growing space in a greenhouse or outside. Because of the fact that it has really good air circulation it helps to reduce insect and disease problems. Mostly the plant and the produce never come in contact with the ground which eliminates some cleaning of the harvested vegetables.

This type of growing has especially become popular in greenhouses where space may be at a premium. Things like tomatoes, eggplant, cucumbers and peppers thrive in such an arrangement and environment.

There are all types of containers than can be stacked vertically and grown in. Plastic pots, felt and plastic bags and other containers can be used to grow in. See the section on Grow Bags in this book. Things that vine like squash, cucumbers, pumpkins and other vine crops can be vertically grown as long as they have enough room to expand and there is enough soil to support their nutrient needs.

The picture below is licensed under the Creative Commons Attribution-Share Alike 4.0 International license.

Vertical hydroponic gardens of lettuce at University of Florida Research Extension Center Florida

Growing Potatoes

Growing potatoes are an essential skill needed during the Super Grand Solar Minimum. Potatoes are Nutritious and good for you as you can see below. Potatoes can provide much of the nutrition your body needs on a daily basis. Just think, one medium sized potato can delivers 110 fat-free calories. When it comes to vitamins, there is this:

- 45% of your daily need for vitamin C
- 18% of needed potassium
- 10% of vitamin B6
- 8% of vitamin B1 and B3
- And 6% of your needs for iron, folate, phosphorus and magnesium.
- And on and on.

Stealth Potatoes

Other things that are good about potatoes are that they can be grown in a stealth method. The potatoes are not above ground, so they could be grown all over the place and unless they knew about what potato plants look like they would not even know they were there. Also, the potatoes keep underground if there are no insects or it keeps dry. So you can then harvest potatoes months after the above ground part is dead and dry or you have cut and removed them.

Types of Potatoes

You can usually get your seed potatoes at Local nurseries usually have perhaps three types available. If you want more variety you will probably have to go online or over the telephone. It will be a good idea to order early (in the wintertime) for the best selection as potatoes are normally shipped in March or April. If you get them early you can keep them in a dry and cool location until you are ready to plant in the springtime. My favorite is ordering from Fedco Seeds at Moose Tubers: www.fedcoseeds.com/moose.htm. I have used them for years and they provide seeds and equipment as well. Other reputable providers can supply them over the phone or over the internet. There are some potatoes that do well in cold climates. Do some research on the internet. Potatoes have been selectively bred to produce all sorts of flesh colors including gold, red, and blue varieties. The author like the standard Irish (white Russet) potato. My wife likes the red (new Potatoes) and Yukon Gold types. The Russet potatoes are the largest.

SEED POTATOES

A seed potato is a potato that has been grown to be replanted to produce a potato crop. In spring, potato tubers will start to sprout new growth from growing points called eyes. Cut these eyes is large chunks off the sprouted potatao (2 to 2 ½ chunks inch or larger). These sprouted eyes are what is planted.

Growing Potatoes

The author is by no means an expert, but I have grown potatoes for years. I hate digging in the soil but some do. The old tried and true method is to dig up the soil into rows. Then dig back the row and place a seed potato and then cover. You should water well the dug back row before placing the seed potato. After the seed potato sprouts with leaves and a stem, heap compost or more soil over the plant until you are tired or run out of soil. This method provides soil for the new potatoes to expand into. Water but do not over water. Potatoes are somewhat forgiving.

The Authors method

Create a Ruth Stout Garden – See Ruth Stout garden in this book. My potato bed is four foot wide and about 100 ft. long. The hay (about a foot of it or a little more is pulled back to the sides of the four foot bed. The composted soil below the hay is then exposed. I then water the compost and let the water settle in. Then I place a seed potatoes every 6 to 8 inches across the bed and about every 14 or so inches down the 100 foot bed. Yes that's a lot of seed potatoes. After placing all the seed potatoes I recover with the hay I have pulled back. I keep the potatoes watered if necessary. Just dig beneath the hay and check the compost for moisture. I plant in February here in Central Texas and harvest in June. If you need some small potatoes just dig into the hay and snatch a few for your dinner. I am still eating harvested potatoes that I harvested 7 months ago. I am also keeping some of them for seed for next year's planting. Now that's what I call Easy! Please note if the hay composts too fast, just add more hay. And keep lightly watered. Additionally you can use raked leaves for the topping of the bed, but hay really work well. Also if you have really good compost (I use horse manure) then you will never have a need for fertilizer. In fact as you grow in this garden year after year it will only get better.

Harvesting and Storing Potatoes

   Harvesting potatoes can be a child's treasure hunt. Let the kids harvest if possible as it can be a joy to watch as they discover potato after potato. After harvesting, lay out on a dry tarp and let the skins dry. Depending on the temperature this may only take at most a day. After that you can store the potatoes in paper bags in your house which should be a dark cool place if possible. Some people wrap their potatoes in paper before storing. Just be sure that the skins are completely dry. My wife likes to place the potatoes in short paper boxes that soft drinks come in and then keeps them in our wash rood. You can also store them in a produce container in a refrigerator. From the times when there was no refrigeration, potatoes were stored in a covered shed with dry sand covering the ground, The shed protected the potatoes from rain, wind and the sun. The potatoes were laid in the dry sand. Some of course eventually rotted, but most did not and at the next season were used for seed potatoes if they had not been eaten.

Growing Carrots

Carrots are another good SGSM root plant to grow. Carrots can even overwinter if not harvested right away. Just keep them from freezing. Obviously you will need some deep sandy or soft soil unless you grow some of the smaller size carrots. Personally I think the smaller ones are tastier. Carrots don't need a lot of rich organic soils as they will not grow vertically but search out around them for nutrients and not down.

Carrots are very easy to grow as long as you plant them in soil that is deep, sandy and loose. If not your carrots will end up looking like strange creatures. Carrots can tolerate frost and depending on the cultivar may take from 2 to 4 months to mature. Carrots come in a lot of different color and of course sizes.

Here are some tips:

- Your soil should be soft (and perhaps sandy) down to 12 inches.
- Don't add nitrogen or manure rich fertilizers
- Purchase some sand to add to your soil if it needs fluffing up. Carrots don't grow well in clay or rocky soil

Planting Carrot Seed

- You cannot transplant carrots and the seed should just be sprinkled on the groun and sown ¾ inches below the top of the soil and 3 or so inches from each other.
- Sow the seeds 3 to 5 weeks before the last frost date. If planting in rows, they can be from 5 up to 12 inches apart.
- If you want a continuous supply plant every three weeks through the season
- Water often, but don't drown the plant. Shallow watering is better.
- Make sure that there is not a crust that forms by watering which will inhibit germination
- Carrots can be slow growers and may take up to three weeks before you start seeing results

Harvest/Storage

- Harvest when they are large enough for your purposes
- Harvest in the cool part of the day
- Carrots have more sugar available if harvested after a front
- To store. Pull and clean clean and put them in plastic bags in a refrigerator. Remove tops off up to one inch of the top of the carrots body.
- You can also store long time by placing in in dry sawdust in a cool try place like a cellar or root cellar.

TIP – To grow carrots for seed, leave in the ground and next spring they will sprout, flower and produce seeds. Takes two seasons.

Remember carrots are really a healthy and easy to grow vegetable.

Growing Jerusalem Artichokes

Jerusalem Artichokes are another great stealth food plant like potatoes. Nice pretty flowers above ground but below are the wonderful tubers that may be eaten.

Jerusalem artichokes can be planted in the fall, or in spring six to eight weeks before your last frost date. Either way works fine. Make sure each tuber you'll be planting has at least one "eye." Plant them three inches deep and about a foot apart.

The plant is a perennial sunflower native to North America and its tubers are really tasty

They can be eaten raw, put into salads. They remind me of water chestnuts. Like a potato, the flesh browns easily and, after peeling, tubers should be sprinkled with lemon juice and water.

Creative Commons Attribution-Share Alike 3.0 Unported license.

This wonderful tuber can be used in a soup mixed with other vegetables, or just boiled or roasted

Roots of the Jerusalem artichoke

By H2ase - Own work, CC BY-SA 3.0, https://commons.wikimedia.org/w/index.php?cur id=24805030

Harvest after the first frost as the above part of the plant dies back. One great thing about them is you can just store them in the ground and harvest when needed although you can store in a refrigerator, If your ground freezes, place a heavy mulch above them.

The Jerusalem artichoke can become a pest as they tend to spread out. YES that's a real problem as they are underground food, so it's not necessary to dig them all up if you've created a permanent bed for them. Just make sure to harvest and replant if necessary every year. Harvesting prevents congestion of the roots and insures a nice looking tuber.

Order your tuber starts from seed companies. Sometimes these tubers show up in grocery stores and may be used. Once you get some growing, you will have a good source year after year.

The tubers grow in just about any soil but if you grow them in improved soil you will give better results as in more tubers. Adding compost to the plant as it goes will also add to a better soil. Water but do not flood the plant. These plants are very forgiving when it comes to watering.

Greenhouses

Commercial economy Greenhouses

The hoop house on the left is from Growers Supply. This is an easy way to get started. You can enhance this simple hoop house by adding a back and front. This is a good starter greenhouse. Click on image to see more.

Choose from a large selection of frame widths and lengths. Hoop building frames are made from 19 gauge, 1.05" OD USA-made, triple-galvanized structural steel tubing, with 5' rafter spacing and one purlin.

This is the commercial greenhouse I grow in. It is also from Growers Supply.

The following is information from their web site: Extend your growing season with a GrowSpan Round Economy High Tunnel. High Tunnels, also called hoop buildings, are ideal for vegetables, small fruit and cut flowers. Increase yield, enhance quality by 50%!

Manufactured from 14 gauge USA-made, triple-galvanized structural steel tubing.

6' rafter spacing.

6 mil 4 year single layer greenhouse film, for cover and ends, comes complete with all hardware necessary for installation.

Universal Joint Roll-Up for sides, including all hardware. Heavy-duty ground posts included. Click on the image for more information.

Greenhouses - Build your own

I have built a couple of greenhouses in the last few years, and was very happy with the results and how easy it was. Another thing that I liked was that I could customize the length and size I wanted. The following is where I originally purchased the hoop benders that formed the hoops of my greenhouse.
They worked wonderfully.

Build Your Own Greenhouse
Lost Creek Greenhouse Systems
245 C.R. 2651
Mineola, TX. 75773
There excellent website is at this URL
Note all graphics on this page are (C) Lost Creek Greenhouse Systems.

So why am I pushing greenhouses in this blog? The main reason is that soon, only those who posses some form of protection for their crops will be successful at doing so. I have used a greenhouse to grow everything from Tomatoes to microgreens for the last 12 years and have never had a failure except for being blow away by tornadic winds. That happened to my large 30 by 90 foot greenhouse. My smaller one which I built with the bender survived just fine. I could list all types of advantages of using a greenhouse. Here are just a few:

- Season Extension - grow earlier and later into the spring and fall.
- Protection from wind, rain and snow.
- Protection from birds and some insects.
- A controlled environment.
- Fewer weeds
- Great for growing starts that would be harmed by frost and cold weather.

Below is a picture of a hoop bender mounted on plywood. I mounted mine on plywood and put it in the back of my truck to hold it. That worked great.

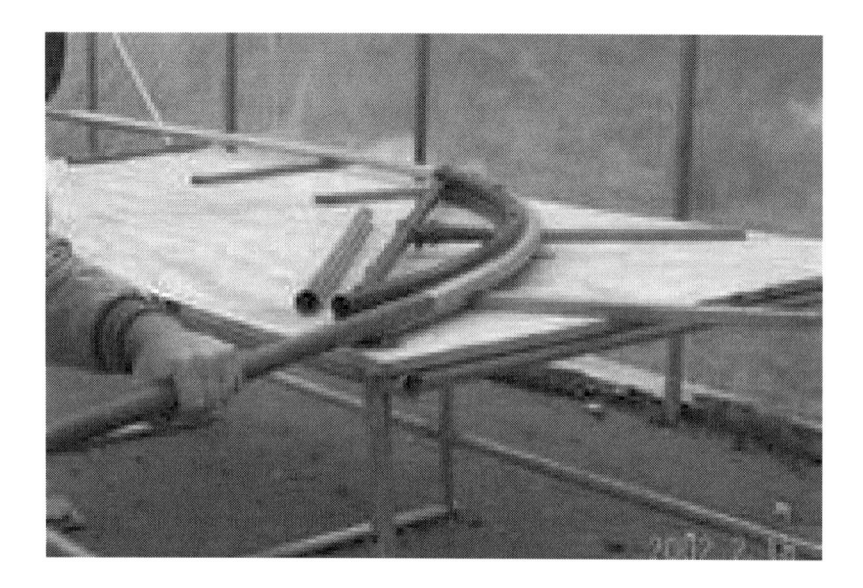

This alone will give you a jump on getting plants producing at the optimum times available. Because of the Super Grand Solar Minimum, we should see our growing seasons compressed. Getting almost full grown starts out in say your Ruth Stout garden will quickly produce food.

TIP: with the proper application of plastic, hay and other materials, it is possible to grow greens in very cold temperatures in a green house. Brassicas (cabbage family) especially do well.

So heads up on greenhouses. This could also become a SGSM business if you would like, I see a huge future in greenhouses as we see our major mono-culture food system fail due to our coming cooler times.

Hydroponic Nutrients

Here is a good source for bulk bags of min in water hydroponic fertilizers. I have used these for years and have really good results. The company is Hydro Gardens and their product is Chem-Gro. If you use their hydroponic formula, you will need Epson salt as an added element. You want get that at Walmart, just make sure it is pure Epson salt. They have mixing instructions at the website. Tip: Don't purchase that expensive liquid fertilizer at a hydroponic shop.

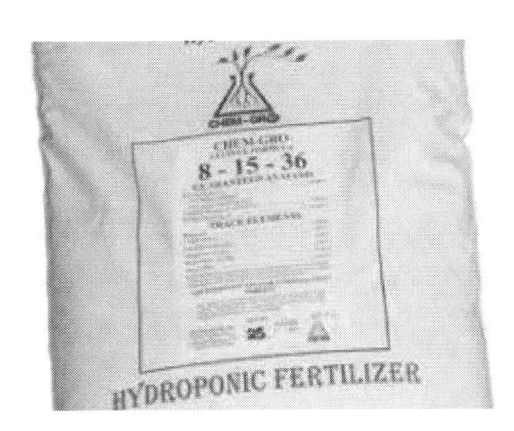

Information on the Author – Dennis DeLaurier

Here is information on me:

My Picture below. I am 76 years old.

A note about the Author

My name is Dennis DeLaurier. There is nothing special about me. I never attended college, received a Masters or Doctors degree and my high school English teachers who are probably all dead (I am 75) suffered an absolute failure to teach me how to use the English language. With that said, please understand that this book contains my own words, and my grammar may leave things lacking as well as my scientific explanations which may be a bit crude.

Things that I have done in my life

Ham Radio Operator, Scout Master, Non-degree Petrophysics, Engineer, Radar technician, Electronics Technician, Trainer and Teacher, Global Server and Storage Support Engineer, Farmer, Father, Grandfather, Hydroponics Grower and I run a Microgreens business. Last but not least in really bad financial times I was a simple Janitor! Of all the occupations, the Janitor part taught me humility and appreciation of people around me. Thank you for purchasing this book. I hope it makes you think. and you very quickly You can find all about me at this URL and the books and courses I sell.

My Blog is at this URL

Printed in Poland
by Amazon Fulfillment
Poland Sp. z o.o., Wrocław